Aloha Spirit:
The True Essence of Hawaiian Spirituality

Kahu
Robert Kalama Frutos

Text by Kahu Robert Kalama Frutos

Copyright © 2014 by Kahu Robert Kalama Frutos.

All rights reserved. ISBN-13: 978-1500991869

Second Edition   ePub ISBN-10: 1500991864

Also by Robert Kalama Frutos;

Hawai'i Sacred Sites of the Big Island Places of Presence, Healing & Wisdom

Hawai'i the Most Beautiful Places to Visit on the Big Island

Day Hikes in Hawai'i Volcanoes National Park: The Best Places to See the Unusual, Find the Unexpected, and Experience the Magnificent!

A Photographer's Guide to the Big Island: Being in the Right Place, at the Right time, for the Best Image

See full list of titles by Robert Frutos on Page 6

www.hawaiisacredsitestours.com

www.hawaiiphototours.org

www.robertfrutos.com

Join me in Hawai'i for a Sacred Site Tour

email: **rfphoto3@gmail.com**   808 345 – 7179

Dedication

You are Spirit Greatness!

To the Lumerian Seed Carriers

&

To all sincere spiritual aspirants, awaking, recalibrating, and stepping into the wonder and magnificence of the realm of Spirit

Aloha and Welcome!

Mahalo Nui Loa!
(With Special Thanks)
to
Kahuna High Priestess Kalei'iliahi

My spiritual sister,
wisdom keeper, visionary artist, seer,
healer, channel, and keeper of Lumerian Truths

&

Kumu Hula Ali'i Kahuna Nui Ehulani

who perpetuates and cultivates
the ancient Hawaiian traditions and culture
with impassioned dedication
and wholehearted commitment...

Kahuna(s) Kale'iliahi & Ehulani

All Photos by Robert Kalama Frutos

Table of Context

A Note about the Creation of this Book   Page 7

Introduction   Page 9

1 Hawaiian Spirituality –
You are Spirit Greatness   Page 15

2 Origin of the Aloha Spirit
  Part 1   Page 19

3 Origin of the Aloha Spirit
  Part 2   Page 25

4 The Motherland Kapapahanaumokukui -
kahikina, later known as Mu   Page 29

5 Mu also known as Lumeria   Page 31

6 Keawe The Eternal Creator
& the Four Major Hawaiian Gods   Page 39

7 1200 A. D. The Time of Drastic Change   Page 51

8 Kukailimoku and the Sacred Ku Stone   Page 57

9 Hidden Years of Hawaiian Spirituality
& Religious Traditions   Page 67

10 1778 – 1874 The Years of Great Adversity   Page 71

11 King David Kalākaua
   A Breath of Life to the Hawaiian Spirit   Page 81

12 Queen Lili'uokalani
   & the Overthrow of the Hawaiian Kingdom   Page 87

13 1900 – 1959
   The Territory Years of Hawai'i   Page 93

14 The Hawaiian Renaissance   Page 97

15 The Awakening… Into the Now!   Page 115

16 To Enhance, Enrich & Deepen…   Page 121

17 The Intent of this Book…   Page 133

   Bibliography   Page 137

   About the Author   Page 139

   Other Books by Robert Frutos   Page 143

A Note About the Creation of this Book...

This book was created by request.
A number of individuals approached me after reading: **Hawai'i Sacred Sites of the Big Island: Places of Wisdom, Healing, and Presence**, and asked me to write a book that specifically shared the deeper significance, and teachings of Hawaiian spirituality, after finding the Sacred Sites book so informative, valuable, and easy to use.

**Aloha Spirit!
The Essence of Hawaiian Spirituality**
is the result.

As the title implies, it shares the true Spirit of Aloha (and its origins) as well as the true essence of Hawaiian spirituality. Some of the same information is shared in **Hawai'i Sacred Sites of the Big Island: Places of Wisdom, Healing, and Presence**,

It has to be – the Aloha Spirit and essence of Hawaiian spirituality is not about a specific person, or on the highest level, about a place, but rather about a consciousness, a state of awareness, and a way of being. A recognition that Spirit is alive, thriving, and radiantly present.

This book is specifically for those who want to understand, integrate, and aspire to cultivate and/or live... true Hawaiian Spirituality, the universal and profound teachings as they were once known and practiced for more than 20,000 years.

If you are interested in visiting the powerful Sacred Sites of the Big Island and drawing upon their powerful energies and Presence then – **Hawai'i Sacred Sites of the Big Island: Places of Wisdom, Healing, and Presence**, will serve you well.

**If you are seeking, a true understanding and insights into the Aloha Spirit,
and the True Essence of Hawaiian Spirituality** *this* **is the book for you.**

Introduction

"We were not blessed with gold or silver

or gemstones, or unlimited resources

here in Hawai'i,

we were blessed with ALOHA,

and this is our gift to the world."

~ Uncle George Lanakilakekiahialii Na'ope

Hawai'i is one of the most powerful, active
and sacred places on the planet...
where the spirit world is both radiant and present.

A spirit that is felt, both in the love and liveliness
of its people, AND as a living breathing vitality
that permeates the landscape.

Hawai'i is not so much a mere group of islands in
the middle of the Pacific Ocean...

it is a living, breathing Presence,

revealed to those who take the time

to still their minds, open their hearts,

and become receptive to the experience

of both the energy and spirit –

that the Spirit of Aloha sanctions.

It is through respect and receptivity alone, that Hawai'i begins to reveal Her true secrets.

As in any culture, traditions are passed down from generation to generation. And the island heritage for the Hawaiian people was born of, and remains permeated with Aloha!

Aloha means many things to many people - a heartfelt greeting, a blessing, an expression of love.

But on the deepest level, Aloha translates as Alo, "the presence of God with us," and ha translates as "breath." When Alo and ha are put together into one word - the significant meaning becomes "**the Breath of God is in Our Presence**."

*So the fullest expression and radiance of Aloha, comes from our individual inner awareness and recognition that the **Divine Presence** is within each of us, AND within **ALL** things.*

This is the essence & core

of Hawaiian spirituality.

Hawaiian lifestyle, cosmology, and consciousness, recognize that Spirit dwells in ALL things and permeates all life. That Spirit's presence lives and breathes in all things - people, animals, plants, rocks, water, the stars, and the heavens.

Each has their own level of consciousness, and each has their own gift to offer and unique role to play. In Hawaiian conciousness this awareness *IS* recognized, honored, and deeply respected.

To those with quiet minds and open hearts

Spirit's Presence can be found...

in the gentle beauty of a sunrise,

the rhythmic lull of lapping waves,

the healing rays of a tropical sun,

and the powerful displays of Pele's lava

flowing into the sea,

where Spirit declares

its breathtaking wonder

and reveals its awesome power.

For those with eyes to see - Spirit's Presence is consistanly intertwined and radiating within all things.

If viewed and understood from this

perspective, life itself takes on a deeper and more meaningful significance: one that naturally includes great gratitude, unending wonder, and ever-deepening respect - for both Spirit's radiant presence and all life.

With this awareness, life becomes a balance of thriving gratefulness, and grace, and we gain the understanding that we are here simply to love and be loved... to share our gifts, and to live our lives in an inspired, uplifting, and giving way. In doing so, our lives become complete and blessed indeed.

One inspired distinction of the Hawaiian culture is that it is a culture of giving, born of the Aloha Spirit, born of a generous heart, born of the awareness and understanding that ALL comes from the source of unending joy and abundance: Spirit!

Unlike cultures based on the concept of getting something for giving something (commonly referred to as commerce or capitalism) the Hawaiian way of being is to simply give, and to give generously, *knowing that in giving, the giver is receiving the greatest gift of all - inner happiness.*

Another inspired distinction of the Hawaiian culture, is their intimate knowledge of, and great love for the natural world (this can only make sense given the awareness that Spirit lives in all things). Their wisdom (in relationship to nature) garnered through the centuries, has allowed them to both flourish and prosper.

Through the use and understanding of astronomy, weather patterns, fishing mastery, agricultural expertise, healing skills and warfare proficiency, Hawaiians were profoundly adept at the art of living.

With a balanced integration of love and laughter, combined with celebrations, and yearly rituals, and an intimate and cherished perception of their immediate environment, they succeeded in creating a way of living that was balanced, harmonious and filled with unity.

Mixed with the equal godsend of tropical temperatures, and unimaginable natural beauty - life was celebrated with gratitude, through oli (song) hula (dance) pule (prayer) and merriment.

The Aloha path is open to any one...

it simply requires deep sincerity, a quiet mind and an open heart!

A quiet mind forfeits the usual preoccupations of the mind,

and an open heart allows one receptivity and sanctions an intiuitve state of awareness,

all together, this allows you to be fully present and receptive.

This allows you to have an ever-deeping experience that puts you in touch with the deepest, most sacred parts of your inner Self and something so much larger than yourself – an undeniable growing sense of a living radiant Presence.

Danny Akaka, Hawaiian cultural advisor/historian, and kahu (keeper of traditions) shares that the best way to gain the richest and deepest experience while in Hawai'i,

is first, to just simply, slow down.

As you let yourself fully relax, you begin to become aware of all the beauty and mana (energy/power) that permeates the Hawaiian islands.

Being relaxed, allows you to see life from a different point of view, and further, allows you to feel open and receptive to the wonder and beauty of all life.

Only when in a relaxed, receptive, and intuitive state of awareness, will you begin to experience the Aloha Spirit in the deepest way possible.

1

Hawaiian Spirituality
You are Spirit Greatness!

Imagine living in a world full with harmony, cooperation, balance, *and* love.

A world where everything flows unceasingly in a supportive and helpful manner.

A inspiring world created for your own highest good. Where everything works to inspire you to live your best life possible.

Where people love you, appreciate you, and respect you, and offer comfort and guidance when needed or requested.

A world in which everyone is fully aware that Spirit permeates all life, that Spirit's presence lives and breathes in all things - people, animals, plants, rocks, water, the stars and the heavens. That Spirit's presence is intertwined and radiating within all things.

Imagine every person a valued friend rather than stranger or a potential danger,

a community of people all doing their very best to add their gift towards everyone's highest benefit.

A world where laughter and kindness

flow freely and without reservation.

Where much time is put aside for joyous celebration, merriment, storytelling, spending time with loved ones and family, all those near and dear.

Where everything is recognized as a gift from the Creator, and gratitude for the Creator is abundant and without end.

And that we are all caretakers of all Spirit has given us - and we are fully committed to sharing and protecting the productivity and fruitfulness of these gifts.

Imagine that this world is a place of unceasing wonder and extraordinary beauty.

The above description is a true account of - a once lived - way of being... it was an early Hawaiian (Mu) way of living and being, filled with gratitude, beauty, honoring, and the Aloha Spirit.

A life lived with a balanced integration of love and laughter, combined with celebrations, and yearly rituals, and an intimate and cherished perception of one's immediate environment, that succeeded in creating a way of living and being that lasted more than 20,000 years, and that was completely harmonious... full with inner and outer unity.

This way of being continued up until around 1,000 B.C., only a mere 3,000 years ago

What we see in present day Hawai'i are mere remnants... small remaining pieces of a much larger reality, surviving traces of not just a culture, but a continent nation that created a way of living in harmony, cooperation, and balance based on the Aloha Spirit.

Could this all be just a distant dream?
A long lost memory?
A secret hope for the future?
Can it possibly ever have existed?

According to the ancient Hawaiian chants, songs, and oral history, which was the Hawaiian way of chronicling and recording *their* true history, it was not only possible, it was ordained and set forth into creation from the highest heavens.

The destiny and the purpose of being on earth, from an Hawaiian (Mu) spiritual perspective, are twofold: 1) *we are to enjoy the beauty of nature* and 2) *we are to realize consciously our spiritual nature through mutual love (the Aloha Spirit!)*

These have been the guiding Hawaiian spiritual principles since the dawn of Hawaiian creation.

Once chanted and sung in ancient temples by priests and priestesses, this wisdom has been passed down via the spoken word through endless cycles of time.

2

Origins of Aloha Spirit!
Part 1

"We actually came into this world as gods.
It's just that we have forgotten who we really are
as well as what it really means."

- Hale Kealohalani Makua

What are the origins of the Aloha Spirit
and the True Essence of Hawaiian Spirituality?

Hale Kealohalani Makua, a highly revered and honored Hawaiian elder, as well as a record keeper of Hawaiian history, culture and traditions, once shared that his memories of Hawaiian history went as far back as 18 million years.

Given this new light on the length and depth of Hawaiian creation and history, we have perhaps been only looking at the small picture.

We have **only** been looking at the historical accounts as westerners have recorded them, which **only** includes up to the last 2000 years at best, rather than viewing the Hawaiian's perspective of an intimate and chronicled oral history.

Let us now look at it from the sources of pure Hawaiian spiritual understanding and perspectives, according to the ancient chants, songs and oral history.

And let us begin with what we do know... That Hawaiian creation and history begins way beyond any known timeline generally understood and accepted, perhaps millions of years.

That their true and pure history IS found in their chants, songs, and oral history.

In being passed down across the ages and through generations of Hawaiian families, there are Hawaiian descendants, both in the past, and living today, whose specific role was/is to carry these traditions, teachings, and wisdom forth.

That NOW, more than any other time, these traditions, teachings, and wisdom, are being allowed to be fully shared - as well as needing to be shared - on a wide-world platform.

Drawing from many living Hawaiians today, be they kahuna, kahu, healers, seers, the light-carriers of Aloha, or have in someway been responsible and entrusted to carry on and share these teachings and wisdom,

as well as drawing upon the ancient Hawaiian chants, songs and oral history, let us begin to create a new understanding of the True Essence of Hawaiian Spirituality from a purely Hawaiian perspective.

If you are ready... be prepared and open for a departure from your usual way of perceiving – for what you may have been introduced to as the genuine and accurate Hawaiian history.

Even for just a little while, suspend and put your knowledge off to the side, as these authentic Hawaiian perspectives and insights, offer a worldview different from the usual idea of what Hawaiian history is, as well as what the majority of people believe today about it. If ready, then...

Welcome
come join us on a journey...
A journey of unutterable beauty
and magnificent wonder,
a journey across the landscapes
of the heart & soul,
where dreams and love and hope are born,
where inspiration, imagination, and creativity reside and know no limits,
where Spirit soars and radiant peace abounds!

Then rejoice in knowing that the primary and foremost principles of True Hawaiian Spirituality as taught and shared by the ancient Hawaiians are as follows:

Everything is a manifestation of Divine energy

Divine energy is not self-existent nor self-created, but comes directly from the mystery known as Aku/Spirit

That the destiny and the purpose of being on earth, are twofold: 1) we are to enjoy the beauty of nature and 2) we are to realize consciously our spiritual nature through mutual love (the Aloha Spirit!)

Our Guardian Spirits are here to show us how to live happily, healthily, and to advance spiritually. Some of these Guardian Spirits have formed the true priesthoods of Hawai'i's ancient spirituality

There are also Guardian Spirits for all other forms of life on this planet, and we should live in harmony with them

The method of creating happiness is through selfless service, which alone truly allows inner joy in the beauty of nature to combine with mutual love. This was/is the way of the real Aloha Spirit of Hawai'i

Included with the above principles, as the basis and source of True Hawaiian Spirituality are an understanding of the positive and negative forces.

The positive power works through the heavenly, while the negative power works through the material.

The positive and negative forces need to be balanced and brought together for completeness.

Through the proper use of meditation (see page 119) the positive and negative poles are balanced, an inner connectedness arises, and inner clarity and light can flow.

Prayer is as important as meditation.
True prayer is offered only to the Supreme God. The Aumakua (ancestral spirit guides) are addressed with respect, but more in the conversational tone of a close relative or close friend.

Meditation in part, can be used as a way to prepare the mind to address God in prayer and the Aumakua through chants.

The Hawaiian's believe that God is reflected in nature. Truth is the reality around us, and that we are in harmony and balance with God when we live in the harmony, balance, and beauty of nature.

The above principles and wisdom form the basis for True Hawaiian Spirituality from a pure Hawaiian perspective and history.

3

Origins of Aloha Spirit!
Part 2

With the spiritual principles revealed in the last chapter, let us move into the pure Hawaiian perspective of the Hawaiian creation origins.

Kumulipo: The Hawaiian Chant of Creation, is the most well-known Hawaiian Creation Story. It is a sweeping epic of spiritual poetry that has survived through the ages.

The chant reveals the astounding creative powers of Gods and Goddesses, and repeatedly soars to ecstatic heights of divine grandeur.

The Kumulipo was the pride and joy of temple priests of the Lono order (the order of kahuna who focus was on Lono, the god of peace, prosperity and fertility) who handed down their masterpiece orally from generation to generation through thousands of years of existence.

It was recorded in writing for the first time about 150 years ago. Although it is readily available in book form, no one has been able to correctly translate it into the English language.

Within the Kumulipo lies the true Hawaiian creation story filled with esoteric meaning - but no western translator has yet been able to reveal its many truths.

On their own merit, they give insight and understanding to the Hawaiian Creation Story, but again, is limited by the knowledge of the westerners who attempted to translate it.

There is also another Hawaiian Creation Story, passed down from generation to generation through eons of time, drawn from the ancient chants and songs, that *are* pure Hawaiian.

Again, if you are ready, and prepared to suspend your usual way of perceiving - for just a little while, this creation story offers a sacred and unique understanding of the Hawaiian Creation Story - from a pure Hawaiian perspective.

In the Hawaiian oral tradition, the seeds for the Aloha Spirit were first planted up to 18 million years ago, and the souls that carried these seeds are primarily from the Pleiadian star system.

The ancient Hawaiians say... "In attempting to envision the debut of souls of mankind from the heavens, one must not think literally of human bodies flowing forth in the breath of life from God."

Rather visualize these emerging souls as the ancient Hawaiians viewed them:

"The Spirits flew hither in a gentle breeze. They came hither in a great river... that flowed from the breast of heaven, and floated away from celestial spheres.

Tiny effervescent sparks, scintillating with phosphorescent brilliance, rising from the soft bluish-white glow which encircles the majestic Spirit of the Infinite – the brightest light in the world, yet the most glorious and soothing to behold."

The above words are from a song about the Hawaiian heritage of earth and its tiny young inhabitants who migrated hither in a gentle breeze that wafted from the Almighty Flame of Creation.

This song was once sung in the temples by priests and priestesses of ancient Hawai'i (Mu). It depicts, most eloquently the native Hawaiian conception of the creation of the souls of mankind.

Hale Kealohalani Makua also shares that some of the first Hawaiian inhabitants were from the Sirius star system as well. That they came down from Sirius in great canoes of light.

These souls from the Pleiadian star system and the Sirius star system were eventually to become the foundation of the earliest race of human beings, who later would organize this world's original civilization.

4

The Motherland Kapapahanaumokukuikahikina
later known as Mu

The original Hawaiian soul inhabitants landed upon the earth on a vast land mass in the Pacific, It was known as Kapapahanaumokukuikahikina, later to become known as the continent of Mu.

The heart of humanity was born on Kapapahanaumokukuikahikina, at a verdant sancuary of tropical luxuriance known as the "Garden of Sunshine."

The ancient native Hawaiian's describe it as a place of giant tree ferns and slender tall bamboo. A site rich with mountain apple trees and the pungent green maile vine, with wild hibiscus flowers which blossomed randomly upon rambling hau trees.

A place where every plant worked in harmony and cooperation with one another and held no fear of predatory assault.

A world of richly plumed birds and bright butterflies flitting in playful flight,
where young leaves of taro and huge bushes of sacred 'ape (ah-pay) were abundant.

Where menuhune, elves, fairies, and water

nymphs froliced with delight, and nature spirits endeavored and strived in cooperation and harmony for the benefit of mankind.

This is where humanity began, where the first human beings emanated, emerged into life, and developed into growth. It is here that the Hawaiian Creation story comes to life.

5

Mu
also known as Lumeria

Mu is an ancient civilization.
Mu is also sometimes referred to, or known as Lemuria, or the Motherland (of Mu).

At the peak of its civilization, the Lemurian people were both highly evolved and spirituallly advanced.

Physically, it existed in the Southern Pacific. The lands belonging to the gigantic continent of Mu once included Hawai'i, Easter Island, the Fiji Islands, Australia and New Zealand.

Also lands in the Indian Ocean and Madagascar. It is said that the most Eastern coast of Mu also extended to parts of British Columbia, and to California, particularly the Los Angeles area.

This would explain why many spiritual people are drawn there and why there has been such an influx of higher consciousness ideas that have come from that part of the west coast.

It is because the vibration of that ancient land which was more femininely based and creatively based is once again moving in the consciousness of our planet.

Awakening of Heart and Absolute Love

The basic teachings of Mu were the principles of a higher power, love (Aloha Spirit) and respect for each other, along with love and respect for the Earth.

That is the very foundation of Mu (Hawaiian) spirituality. That was the spirituality of the ancients and this is the spirituality that needs awakening in this world now!

There was a knowing within every Lemurian that all life was harmonious, balanced, creative, and joyful, and worked through a heart flow rather than the separated mind/head space.

The important concepts were unity, community, awareness, centeredness, respect, absolute love (Aloha Spirit) and love of others (This knowledge was located in the organ of the heart.)

Its purpose was to awaken a person to God consciousness and their soul to a genesis of creating the world they wanted. This was the key. Part of the great knowledge of Mu was that we create our own world.

With this understanding and the ability of telepathic communication, the Lemurians knew that whatever they thought and focused their attention on - would become their truth and their creation.

They knew to take responsibility for their thoughts, actions and reactions. They were able to change anything instantly, and know that if they came from a space and place of heart that all manifestation of love (Aloha Spirit) would come to fruition.

With this knowledge the strongest focus was LOVE, Absolute Love (Aloha Spirit!)

In ancient science, in Mu, the ALCHEMY was to redirect and transform a civilization from being unconscious to conscious, meaning being fully aware of God and our own divinity, as well as being able to create our own world.

Alchemy is the ability to convert and exchange one form for another, or correctly said - is the ability to change matter to another form through the use of human consciousness.

In Mu this was done with the transference of energy from fear to love. This is part of the next evolutionary step of mankind.

ANCIENT KNOWLEDGE IS ABOUT RAISING THE CONSCIOUSNESS

KAHUNA - HUNA

The Kahuna of Hawai'i, were the guardians of Huna, the "profound inner knowledge," from Mu.

In ancient Hawai'i, the Kahuna healed and taught in the spirit and vibration of 'Aloha'. This vibration of spirit manifest through love. The purpose behind the 'Kahuna' teachings was/is the revelation of truth within each individual.

In other words, awakening into self realization through God and ABSOLUTE LOVE (Aloha Spirit!) The wisdom and knowledge of the Kahuna is very ancient, coming directly from the land of Mu.

To gain knowledge, the beings of Mu turned inward to connect with the Divine or UM (Universal Mind) through meditation and concentration.

The wise ones had great faith and trust in the Divine and in themselves as manifestations of the one Cosmic Mind. They were able to directly tap into it as GOD, "the source."

In Mu the teachings were pure, balanced and honored. The teachings and principles of Huna are still taught today. The goal being to transcend the body and mind into higher awareness and the frequency of love (Aloha Spirit.)

The principles of Huna are directly from the source of Mu. The teachings from Lemuria were from GOD about God and how to connect back to God.

It is said that the seven sisters (from the Pleiadian

star system) came to earth to assist us in seeding our divinity.

That lineage eventually developed into the inner wisdom and an inner spirituality that there was only ABSOLUTE LOVE (Aloha Spirit!)

MU was/is about the transformation of the human soul, the ending of all dualities, to be made whole and complete again, as we once were.

It is shared that the culture of the inhabitants of Mu was one of peace, love (Aloha Spirit) harmony, compassion, prosperity and manifestation.

Because communication was all telepathic there was little need to speak. Everyone would get the same image, feeling or knowing. The bonus of this was oneness of consciousness.

Language was of light or in every day language absolute love. This language was in sound and wavelengths and vibrated as one. Brain waves were also one *and access to potentiality was there at all times.*

The most powerful communication was the connection to crystals and storage of information in these crystals. Crystals were like our modern day computers but had more power, more knowledge and were totally natural.

One of the regular ceremonies performed was

gathering around a large crystal and creating a connection with the heart and to the sound level of that crystal - which represented the matrix of all creation.

Much of the Mu civilization lived in homes with transparent roofs. They were free from stress and disease, lived to be one to two thousand years old, and developed their telepathic abilities through many thousands of years of societal practice and experimentation.

With many centuries of evolution, the Mu gained telepathy, astral travel and teleportation... making land vehicles unnecessary.

The inhabitants of Mu were primarily a vegetarian, agricultural, outdoor, organic culture that worked in harmony with nature and the land, having little use for scientific technology. Rather they had concentrated on meditation and extra sensory perception (ESP) development.

Although they did use sonic ultra-high frequencies, solar energy, crystal energy, and teleportation to build and move objects.

Mu was a tropical, feminine based society.
It had central places where there were groups of clairvoyant seers, oracles and holy people doing healing and sound work.

There were no power struggles in Mu - as true power was recognized as Absolute Love (Aloha Spirit!)

There were 350 million Lemurians through time, and they lived in ABSOLUTE PEACE, LOVE AND HARMONY (Aloha Spirit) for more than 20,000 years.

Their souls carry within them a Lemurian seed. A seed that allows them to remember that time when peace and love and harmony prevailed upon this earth, and also allows them to reawaken into the full magnificence of their divinity, sharing with others these wisdoms and the true Aloha Spirit.

After 185,000 years of existence, the glaciers of Mu began to melt. The seers and prophets of Mu knew the melting glaciers would eventually set off a multitude of other catastrophic events (earthquakes and volcanoes.)

They further knew that this would take place in about 5,000 years (about 15,000 years ago) and that Mu would then sink beneath the ocean.

They then began preparations for sending the inhabitants of Mu off in 8 directions, to keep them safe as well as safeguard the ancient wisdom and the true spiritual teachings.

When Mu was destroyed, its people who left before its demise eventually became the Tibetans, the Indians (India) the Eskimos, the Mayans, Africans, Egyptians, Greeks, and the Native Americans.

There were also a number of Mu inhabitants that

chose to stay on Mu through its catastrophic events. Many survived and continued living here (in the Hawaiian islands) generation after generation on through to the present time.

6

Keawe
The Eternal Creator
&
the Four Major Hawaiian Gods

From the earliest chants and songs
Keawe was revealed as **the eternal creator, the supreme being**

He was known by a number of names including 'Io, (Ee-oh) which means "soul, one's genuine inner self," and the "I am Spirit" in man.

He was known as Ke Kumu Nui (the Great Teacher) who enlightened faithful devotees with divine truths and wisdom of spirit.

He was known as Akua Hoho which means the indwelling Spirit of God; the god who is one's intimate companion.

And He was sometimes referred to as Ke Akua Ulu, which means the God of inspiration, as well as the God who breathed life into existence and infused the Spirit of Himself into the offspring of his divine creatures.

Keawe the Eternal Creator was sometimes called I'ao (Ee-yah-o) which means Infinite Light, Infinite World. Keawe was the Supreme Light of the World.

Keawe Creates the World

In the beginning Po was a vast, empty land, a dark abyss where only one life form dwelled. This was the spirit of Keawe. A single light shone through the darkness of Po - a flame holding the energy of creation.

In this chaotic vortex, Keawe evolved order. He opened his great calabash and flung the lid into the air. As it unfolded, it became the huge canopy of blue sky. From his calabash, Keawe drew an orange disk, hanging it from the sky to become the sun.

Next Keawe manifested himself as Na' Wahine, a female divinity considered his daughter. She is also **known as Uli - the highest manifestation of Divine universal feminine energy, the Goddess of Serenity.**

In the beginning, from the earliest oral Hawaiian chants and songs through hundreds of thousands of years - up until around only 3,000 years ago, there was only one main god and one goddess ever worshipped – 'Io & Uli.

The multitude of gods that eventually came into being and are now the known residing and present gods of Hawai'i, including the 4 major Hawaiian gods: Kāne, Ku, Lono, and Kanaloa, as well as the other 1000's of gods, came into dominance much later.

Up until 3,000 years back, the focus and emphasis of Hawaiian spirituality was the Divine Feminine.

It was a time when women were highly regarded and cherished, and were known and honored as the givers or bringers of life.

The high priestesses were immensely esteemed and revered, and viewed as models of purity and virtue. So highly honored were they, that they were included in every ceremony and celebration and were often given priority of importance.

It was around 1,000 B.C. that everything shifted from a focus on the Divine Feminine to a male dominated society and a refocus on the male gods.

What brought this shift of focus into place?

Viewing the long ranging patterns of time, we cycle from ascending to descending levels of awareness, and then cycle back again from descending to ascending levels of consciousness.

From the lowest levels of awareness, known as the dark ages, where goodness and virtue all but disappear from the earth, to the golden age where the highest levels of consciousness prevail and manifest as a dynamic, pulsating harmony, balance, beauty, and love. As well as the individual conscious awareness of being one in god.

These cycles are known by many names, they have been called many things, the wheel of time, the yugas, the iron age, the bronze age, the silver age, the golden age, to name a few. They were "discovered" and known by many cultures: the Greeks, the Mayans, and in India, for example.

And at the end or beginning of each cycle, human consciousness shifts towards higher awareness or lower awareness depending on the point of time in the cycle. It was 3,000 years ago that mankind was at one of the lowest points of awareness.

This would explain and give credence as to why the major shift from a focus on the Divine Feminine to a male dominated society happened along with a refocus on the male gods, and especially Ku, the war god.

Mankind would have simply slipped from a time of higher consciousness, to a lower consciousness. From a time of great peace and harmony to a time of war and bloodshed.

This would give insight as to why the early immigrants (considered the first migration to Hawai'i as recorded by westerners) were not a peace loving people, and in fact, came from distant islands that were at constant war with one another.

This would make clear why the early years of Hawai'i (between 1,500 and 2,000 years back) were constantly filled with battles of dominance for supremacy, over lands, territories, and islands, and why there was the bloodshed of human sacrifice from 1199 A.D. right up until the death of Kamehameha I in 1819.

Bringing it all back around into context then... in the beginning there was only one supreme God known as Keawe, and only one Goddess, Uli, who were the focus of worship.

Next Keawe manifested himself as Kāne, his own son, also known as Eli or Eli-Eli, who was the male generative force of creation.

It is said Na' Wahine (Uli) and Kāne mated spiritually to produce a royal family, who became the additional primary gods worshipped by the Hawaiian people.

In ancient chants and rituals, their three sons: Ku, Lono, and Kanaloa, along with Kāne are the four major Hawaiian gods.

Keawe made Kāne the ruler of natural phenomena, such as the earth, stones, and fresh water.

Ku as Kukailimoku was a god of war, but he also reigned over woodlands and crops, and in various forms was worshipped by craftsmen.

Kanaloa was responsible for the southern Pacific Ocean and as such was god of seamen and the lord of fishermen.

Lono, as lord of wisdom, caused the earth to grow green. As a god of medicine, he was responsible for overseeing the flourishing of herbs and medicinal plants. Lono was the god who presided over the makahiki season (the 4 month celebration usually from October to February) when all war ceased and taxes were paid to the ali'i.

Kāne and Na' Wahine (Uli) also had daughters. Among them, Laka was the goddess of hula; Hina was the goddess of the moon and also the mother of the demi-god Maui; and Kapo, the goddess of the South Pacific who was largely worshipped on Maui (see more about the 4 main Hawaiian gods at the end of this chapter.)

The Freedom to Worship

To bring us into recent Hawaiian history... from 1,500 to 2,000 years back, this is a picture of how spirituality was lived and practiced during those years, and the role of the four major gods of Hawai'i.

Each person worshipped a deity, or akua (god) that represented their profession. Gods existed for bird snarers, canoe makers, robbers, kapa makers, fishermen, etc.

Most farmers revered Lono, who was considered a benign god. When crops ripened, farmers performed religious services to the gods by building a fire to honor whichever god they worshipped, be it Ku, Kane, Lono, or Kanaloa.

During the ceremony, food was cooked and portioned out to each man who sat in a circle around an idol of that particular god. A kahuna offered the food to heaven.

After the ceremony was completed, the people could eat freely of the cooked food, but each time new food was cooked in the imu (underground oven), a bit of it had to be offered to the god again before the common man could eat.

Interestingly, commoners could freely worship their personal gods, voicing their own prayers. For the ali'i (royalty), however, a kahu-akua, who was a priest or keeper of the idol, uttered the prayer.

The highest chief was the only one allowed to command the construction of a luakini (sacrificial) heiau (Hawaiian Temple) to honor Kukailimoku, the war god, which required sacrificial offerings of human life during its construction.

Lesser chiefs could build mapele, stone temples, to invoke the blessing of gods like Lono who could insure abundant crops.

These temples were surrounded with posts carved with images, while inside idols carved of wood, stone or sea urchin spines, or fashioned of feathers attached to woven i'e i'e netting represented various gods.

Oracle towers that jutted 20 feet into the sky held offerings made to the gods on wooden platforms far above the ground.

The Four Hundred, the Forty Thousand, and the Four Hundred Thousand Gods

Over time Kāne, Ku, Lono and Kanaloa created ALL the lesser gods which became known as The Four Hundred, the Forty Thousand, and the Four Hundred Thousand Gods.

The Kahuna of old were responsible for knowing and reciting each of these 400, 40,000 and 400,000 names of the gods.

They not only had to know their names, but had to know them in proper order of importance, and also know what the appropriate offering was for each god - in order not to offend any of them.

To bring this chapter to conclusion...

Keawe or 'Io was the original and supreme Hawaiian God.

He and then his daughter Na' Wahine, better known as Uli, were the only god and goddess worshipped throughout Hawaiian history up until 1,000 B.C.

It was said that the name of Uli was considered so sacred, it could only be uttered by the highest Kahuna once every generation.

This all changed about 3000 years ago – when the Hawaiian culture and its spirituality shifted from a Divine Feminine focus to a male dominate society with a focus on the 4 dominant male gods.

The gods Kāne, Ku, Lono, and Kanaloa would then prevail as the main religious focus. The Hawaiians would then drift away from Keawe/'Io and Uli worship, into the worship of the four main Hawaiian gods and the Aumakua system.

The 4 Major Hawaiian Gods

Since this book is about the essence of Hawaiian Spirituality, the role it played in their daily lives, and how the Aloha Spirit continues today,

it is important that the readers have at least a little knowledge of who the main gods are of the Polynesian nation and what their relationship is to each other and to man. So each god's role is described and addressed a little more fully below.

Kāne

Kāne is considered the highest of the four major Hawaiian deities along with Ku, Lono and Kanaloa,. He represented the god of procreation and was worshipped as ancestor of chiefs and commoners.

Kāne is the creator and gives life associated with dawn, sun and sky. No human sacrifice or laborious ritual was needed in the worship of Kāne. Kāne is represented by an uncarved upright stone, since it is thought mankind cannot put form to the formless one. Kāne is lord of the West.

Kāne is married to Na'wahine (Uli.) Together Kane and Uli created Kanaloa, Ku, and Lono, their first three sons. They also had three daughters: Kapo, Hina, & Laka, who married Kanaloa, Ku & Lono.

Ku

Ku was the god of prosperity, as well as the much-feared and terrible god of war and sorcery. He was also god of the deep forest, of the mountain, of dry and wet farming and the god of fishing.

Ku and his manifestations such as Kuka'ilimoku (Ku, the snatcher of islands -- the personal god of King Kamehameha I (see chapter 8, Kuka'ilimoku and the Sacred Ku Stone) were brought to Hawai'i by Pa'ao and around that time, Ku became the primary god of Hawaii (1199 A.D.)

Today, Ku is the prevailing deity in the heiau of Hawaii, and so women are not allowed on the platforms of the heiau and are not allowed to make offerings. The days of dishonor to women are over, however, and it is time to end that prohibition. Ku is Lord of the North.

Ku is married to Hina. She is the feminine aspect of Ku. In many situations today, in Hawaii, Hina is invoked in facilitation of the process of healing, since Ku is the presiding deity of many heiau.

Lono

Lono is the god of fertility, agriculture, rainfall, music and also peace.
In one of the many Hawaiian stories of Lono, he is a fertility and music god who descended to Earth on a rainbow to marry Laka.

In agricultural and planting traditions, Lono was identified with rain and food plants. Lono was also the god of peace. In his honor, the great annual festival of Makahiki was held (a four month celebration.) Lono is lord of the East.

Lono is married to Laka. She embodies the feminine aspect of Lono. As one of Pele's most prominent sisters, Laka is the major deity of the Hula. She is also one of the seven sisters of Pele.

Kanaloa

Kanaloa was the god of the ocean, a healer god, and the ruler of Mana, and the close companion of Kane, the god of creation. They would journey together, share the sacred drink of 'awa, and use their staves to strike the ground and cause springs of fresh water to burst forth. Kanaloa is Lord of the South.

Kanaloa is married to Kapo. As such, she becomes the feminine aspect of Kanaloa. Kapo is also one of Pele's seven sisters, and one of the goddesses of the Hula.

Today, though many of the 1,000's of gods may have disappeared from every day life, in many Hawaiian households, they will never be completely forgotten.

7

1199 A. D.
The Time of Drastic Change

From 1,000 B.C. until 1199 A.D. the Hawaiian culture continued to develop and thrive. However, the time of great peace and harmony (Lemuria) had long disappeared.

This created an overlay for an upcoming new Hawaiian culture, based upon the same remaining land mass of Mu.

The Aloha Spirit energy filled with the vitality and vibrancy born from the Lemurian civilization, so permeated the landscape of the Hawaiian islands, that the existing *and* the new incoming inhabitants (considered the first wave of immigrants, 1,500 to 2,000 years ago) naturally absorbed this quality into their lives and culture.

Though the Aloha Spirit energy was paramount for many thousands of years, it was at long last lost sight of - at the very height of the dark ages.

Thus began the years of war and conquest in the Hawaiian islands, leading up to the arrival of Pa'ao and the culmination of human sacrifice and bloodshed.

Human sacrifice was not created by the Hawaiians, but rather forced upon their existing society by outside forces. It eventually became absorbed into their culture, for just over 600 years, until 1819 when King Kamehameha abolished it upon his deathbed.

Around the year 1200 A. D., this new and devastating influence began to overtake the Hawaiian islands.

Pa'ao was a high-priest from Tahiti, who migrated to the Hawaiian Islands near the year 1200 A.D. Under his leadership and influence Hawai'i was to change forever.

Pa'ao and his people sailed by the stars until they reached the Big Island of Hawaii. After a long and arduous journey, where they nearly ran out of provisions, the party of Pa'ao and friends finally reached the shore of a new land.

Pa'ao and his company were greeted with open arms and Pa'ao was pleasantly surprised that these "foreigners" spoke a language similar to his.

Pa'ao and his people, along with new gods, were received with offerings. Food and clothing in abundance were given. Land in Puna, near Hilo, was set apart for their dwelling-place.

He settled down in this environment and eventually became high priest of Hawaii, the highest in priestly rank over all who were dwelling in the Hawaiian islands.

He established a strict religious system,

introducing to Hawai'i the first human sacrifices ever made in these islands. He also introduced and enforced the custom of kapu-o (prostration), the pulo'ulo'u (a royal insignia marking off a kapu area), and the walled heiau (previously, heiau had been open courtyards.)

Pa'ao justified and sanctioned the social order as he created it, with many new laws and rules, which if broken - were punished by penalty of death.

Pa'ao and his priests built a stone temple platform, or heiau, near Kalapana in lower Puna, known Aha-'ula, or "Red-assembly," so named because of the red feather cloaks worn by the god Ku-kaili-moku and the other gods. This was the first luakini heiau in Hawai'i, the first heiau (Hawaiian Temple) where human sacrifices were offered.

He left priests there to care for the temple and to cover the lava rock with soil brought in pandanus baskets from the hill country, to plant rare trees and dig a well, so making an oasis of that desert environment.

Pa'ao was aware that the district chiefs would, before long, ask him to become the high chief. Some of the chiefs had already said, "It may be the will of the gods that the high priest become the high chief also."

But Pa'ao knew his own power. He felt that his position as high priest was unassailable.

He wanted no civil entanglements. He had managed to surround himself with mysteries, and had gained unbound influence through arousing superstitious fears as well as through warlike deeds.

Satisfied with his own heights of power he declined the offer as position of high chief. This decision would prove to be a major turning point in Hawaiian history.

Pa'ao, then sailed back to Tahiti and brought his brother Pilika'aiea, of "pure" ali'i (royal) blood to be high chief. This high chief Pilika'aiea, would eventually prove to be an ancestor of Kamehameha I.

Pili, as he was known, journeyed with what oral tradition recalls as a "cloud of boats." Along with Pili came his family, chiefs, warriors, and priests. It was a migration of a small nation to a distant home. Thus was Pili set apart as High Chief of Hawai'i.

From Hilo, High Chief Pili went to the beautiful Waipio Valley, taking Pa'ao with him. Pa'ao went to Paka'alana heiau, where he built another temple. Here he left two white stones which were worshipped by the inhabitants of that district, especially by the high chief, Liloa.

Later they moved to the Kohala district. Here Pa'ao built the famous Mo'okini heiau, another luakini heiau (human sacrifice temple) in a place to which he gave the name it still bears--Lae Upolu, the Cape of Upolu.

Here, in Kohala, the high priest and the high chief made their home. The priest and the chief stand out from the mists of the past, representing two great forces of Hawaiian government -the religious and the civil. Independent of each other, the rights of each were jealously guarded.

Pa'ao gave Pili no chance for choice. While he granted to the king civil authority, he retained absolute independent control over the minds of the chiefs and the people in religious matters.

Hawaiian attitudes towards the high chiefs have changed; the ancient high chiefs are often seen today as oppressors, invaders who descended upon a peaceful and Hawaiian population.

Activists praise the pre-Pa'ao days as the real Hawaiian past, to be revived and reenacted in the present, and vilify Pa'ao as a source of Hawaiian problems. In this perspective, *many* of the problems faced by Native Hawaiians can be traced to foreign interference.

8

Kukailimoku and the Sacred Ku Stone

The Ku stone was a symbol of Hawai'i's spiritual and priestly traditions from the early 1200's A.D. In oral tradition it is said to have been brought to the Hawaiian islands by Pa'ao himself.

Its importance, is that to generations of kahuna and tribal chiefs, it was the embodiment of power, as whoever held the Ku stone held the people. It was treasured, honored, revered, and highly protected for this reason.

Kuka'ilimoku was one of the many names attributed to the god Ku. Ku has numerous names according to what quality or characteristic he was representing.

Ku was prayed to and invoked for good crops, long life, as well as family and national prosperity, but he is primarily known as the god of war (see names at the end of this chapter.)

Kuka'ilimoku was a specific deity form of the war god Ku, which literally means "snatcher of the islands." Kuka'ilimoku became Hawai'i's war god and was considered the source of Kamehameha's victories.

The actual Ku stone was kept in a temple for safekeeping and was never removed.
The spirit and energy of the Ku stone was prayed into the feathered god deity, and then carried into battle.

Kuka'ilimoku had a prominent place, on the battlefield, in front of the army. Near the king the high priest carried the war god Kuka'ilimoku, elevated on a staff. This feathered god with pearl shell eyes and 94 dogs teeth in his mouth, it was said, would scream.

The sound could be heard emanating during times of war. At one time the god had a crest of feathers that would bristle and point the way into battle. The standing feathers were considered a favorable sign.

*****

It was once a time honored tradition, that when a Hawaiian king was getting ready to depart this world, he would leave his kingdom to his eldest son. This included all his lands, treasures, *and* the war god deity Kuka'ilimoku.

In 1782, chief Kalani'ōpu'u, for reasons unknown, broke with this traditon giving his eldest son Kīwala'ō all his lands and treasures, but leaving the war god deity to Kamehameha his nephew.

Raised in the royal court of his uncle

Kalaniʻōpuʻu, Kamehameha thus achieved a prominent religious position, guardianship of the Hawaiian god of war.

This was a significant choice, as whoever retained guardianship of Kukaʻilimoku, held rulership to all military powers. Thus the potential schism for power to rule Hawaiʻi island was put into place.

This proved to be Kamehameha's greatest opportunity to begin his quest to unite all the Hawaiʻi islands under his rule and leadership.

Soon after he received guardianship of Kukaʻilimoku, Kīwalaʻō and Kamehameha went to battle. Kīwalaʻō's army was defeated and Kīwalaʻō was killed during the conflict.

Thus, bringing the sole rulership to Kamehameha of all Hawaiʻi island - one step closer to fruition. The only remaining chief in the way was Keōua, Kīwalaʻō younger brother.

Keōua was eventually killed in 1791, clearing the path for Kamehameha to become the exclusive ruler of Hawaiʻi island and then all other Hawaiʻī islands.

Throughout his conquest and reign, Kamehameha worshipped his beloved deity, the war god Kukaʻilimoku. He built the massive Puʻukoholā Heiau (Hawaiian Temple) in Kawaihai in Kukaʻilimoku's honor.

He also built another heiau known as Hale o Kaʻili to house Kukaʻilimoku at Holualoa Bay, one of the seven royal compounds near Kona.

And, he built a shrine at his families meditation grounds near Kapanaia bay (not far from Pololu Valley) for Kuka'ilimoku's safekeeping, This shrine was also known as Hale o Ka'ili.

After his complete conquest of the Hawai'i islands in 1812, King Kamehamaha I, returned to the Big Island and made Kamakahonu (in Kona) his home, where he refocused his energy from war to peace.

He rebuilt the 'Ahu'ena Heiau as his personal heiau (temple) and dedicated it as Hale O Lono (House of Lono). Lono is a god of peace, prosperity and fertility.

Help from the gods for the King and his people were invoked at this site through the appropriate rituals and food offerings.

At Kamakahonu there remains the enduring and noticeable qualities of radiant peace and tranquility.

This is perhaps, because it is a heiau of peace and prosperity, perhaps because Kamehameha I spent the last restful years of his life there, or perhaps because the focus of the rituals were for the upliftment of humanity's higher nature.

Whatever the reason, because of Kamehameha's shift of focus from the war god Kuka'ilimoku, to Lono the god of peace, *Kamehameha brought an end to more than 600 years of human sacrifice.*

With the passing of time and prior to his death on May 8, 1819, Kamehameha decreed that his son, Liholiho, would succeed him in power; he also decreed that his nephew, Kekuaokalani, have control of the war god deity Kukaʻilimoku (a similar scenario to Kalaniʻōpuʻu and Kīwalaʻō/Kamehameha.) Again, having two leaders, one as the ruler, and the other is charge of all military powers

Whenever a beloved Hawaiian aliʻi departs from this world, there is a period of bereavement and grace offered to all. It is a time of intense grief and all the kupus (taboos) are put aside allowing anyone and everyone to grieve in such a manner as they see fit.

Anyone who breaks a taboo, is forgiven, whereas in most cases breaking of a taboo would be punishable by death.

Anyone can sleep with whoever they choose without worry of recrimination, stealing or other offences went by unchecked, extended bouts of drunkenness were acceptable.

Whatever it took to allow people to get through their great loss and grief was tolerated, usually for a 6 month period. This was the social clime and state of affairs when a luau (feast) was arranged in Liholiho's honor.

Shortly after the death of Kamehameha I in 1819, his older son Liholiho, now known as Kamehameha II, and his stepmother Ka'ahumanu, the most powerful woman in all Hawai'i at the time, organized a huge luau and invited all the high chiefs and Kahuna in honor and celebration of the new king Kamehameha II.

At this stately dinner, they sat next to each other and ate, this was traditionally an act punishable by death, as there was a strict taboo against men and women eating together.

With this simple act, they intentionally and publicly violated this taboo, with the purpose of changing the social order and destroying the old religion.

They then made a speech to the bewildered crowd telling the people that the old religion was dead, and ordered the destruction of all the heiaus and burning of the idols.

They did so with the permission and approval of Kahuna Nui (High Priest) Hewahewa.

The three most powerful people in Hawaii - Liholiho, Ka'ahumanu, and Hewahewa - had mutually decided to repudiate the stagnant old order established by Kamehameha I and to push Hawai'i into an uncharted future.

Hawaiians now had no religion - no basis at all for morality, or for the authority of the chiefs. Chiefs and commoners, who formerly had prayed dozens of times everyday during their normal activities, now had no gods to pray to, and no sense of for their actions.

This created a division among the Hawaiian people. Some people wanted to keep the traditional religious and social structure, and some people wanted to abandon it.

Kekuaokalani (who had received the war god Ku from Kamehameha) and who was Liholiho's cousin, opposed the dissolution of the kapu system and assumed the responsibility of leading those who opposed its cessation.

These included priests, members of his court and the traditional territorial chiefs of the middle rank.

Kekuaokalani demanded that Liholiho withdraw his edict on abolition of the kapu system. Kamehameha II refused.

After attempts to settle peacefully, war was declared on Kekuaokalani. Arms and ammunition were given out that evening to everyone who was trained in warfare.

The two powerful cousins engaged in the final Hawaiian battle at Kuamoʻo – **a battle for tradition versus the modern.**

In December 1819, just seven months after the death of Kamehameha I, the opposing heirs met in battle on the lava fields south of Keauhou Bay.

Liholiho had more men, more weapons and more wealth to ensure his victory. He sent his prime minister, Kalanimoku, to defeat his cousin.

The first encounter went in favor of Kekuaokalani. The king's army suffered a temporary defeat.

Regrouping his warriors, Kalanimoku fought back and trapped the rebels along the shore in the ahupua'a of Kuamo'o.

Kekuaokalani, and his courageous men fought on. Kekuaokalani having earlier received a wound, fainted and fell and, unable to stand, sat on a fragment of lava, and twice loaded and fired a musket on the advancing party.

Manono, his beloved and courageous wife, fought by his side, with steady and dauntless courage.

He finally fell with a musket-ball through his heart. With a wild scream of despair Manono sprang to his assistance.

But the words had scarcely escaped from her lips, when she received a ball in the left temple - fell upon the lifeless body of her husband, and expired.

Thus died the last great defenders of the Hawaiian gods. They died as nobly as they had lived, and were buried together where they fell on the field of Kuamo'o.

King David Kalakaua shares:
"No characters in Hawaiian history stand forth with a sadder prominence, or add a richer tint to the vanishing chivalry of the race, than Kekuaokalani and his courageous and devoted wife, Manono, **the last defenders in arms of the Hawaiian gods**."

Thus ended the cycle of Hawaiian religious traditions, up to that time.

After the great battle at Kuamo'o, Kuka'ilimoku (the ancestral war god deity) was hidden in a cave in Kona following the overthrow of the kapu system in 1819. It now rests in the Bishop Museum on Oahu.

The sacred Ku Stone, was passed down from generation to generation, eventually it would wind up in the hands of Kahuna Kuamoo, one of Kamehameha's sons.

The Ku Stone was then passed on to Kuamoo's own son, Kaniho, and then to Kahuna David Kaonohiokala Bray, known as Daddy Bray (March 5, 1889 – November 11, 1968.) It too, now rests in the Bishop Museum on Oahu.

Some of the Many Faces and Names of Ku

Here is a list of the various personalities of Ku and their domains in Hawaiian mythology:

Kumoku-haliʻi – land

Kuolonowao – high forest

Kuholoholopali - sliding down steep slopes

Kupulupulu - undergrowth

Kukaohialaka - ohia-lehua tree

Kukaieie - pandanus vine

Kumauna - mountain

Kupaaikeʻe - hollowing the canoe

Kuka-o-o - digging stick

Kukulia - dry farming

Kukeolowalu - wet farming

Fishermen would worship Kuula or Kuulakai for the blessings of an abundant catch.

As god of war, in addition to Kukailimoku, he was also known as:

Kunui-akea - the supreme one

Kukeoloewa - the supporter

Kuhoʻoneʻenuʻu - pulling the earth together

9

The Hidden Years of Hawaiian Spiritual & Religious Traditions

Since the intent of this book is to share the Aloha Spirit: The True Essence of Hawaiian Spirituality, for those interested only in this, you may choose to jump ahead to the chapter, The Awakening... Into the Now.

Up until this point, I have stayed strongly on track of the true wisdoms and understandings of Hawaiian spirituality as perceived from a Hawaiian standpoint.

With the overthrow of the kupu system, anyone who continued to believe and practice spiritual & religious traditions had to carry on in hiding and secrecy. Most of the spiritual & religious traditions as well as hula and kahuna practices were outlawed in 1830.

By absolute necessity, those who continued Hawaiian spiritual practices went underground and were secreted away, until the early 1970s, with few exceptions.

Although outlawed, the spiritual and religious practices and traditions were carried on - mostly by families and individuals whose families before them were responsible for safeguarding the sacred wisdoms and spiritual traditions.

They were responsible for keeping the flame of Spirit alive during the darkest hours, passing down the spiritual teachings, practices and traditions from generation to generation until the early 1970's and 1990's.

It was not until the Hawaiian Renaissance began in the 1960s and 1970s that Hawaiian traditions and spirituality would begin to emerge once again (see the Hawaiian Renaissance chapter.)

King David Kalākaua brought a breath of life to the Hawaiian Spirit in 1874 by encouraging the reemergence of several traditional Hawaiian practices such as hula, chanting, sports, and royal rituals (see chapter King David Kalākaua A Breath of Life to the Hawaiian Spirit.) With his passing however, the above mentioned traditions once again fell out of public favor and view.

And it was not until November 23, 1993, when President Bill Clinton signed the "Apology Resolution" (US Public Law 103-150) that all Hawaiian traditions were allowed to step completely forward into the full light of day and once again sanctioned to be practiced openly in public without fear of social prosecution or criminal charge.

This resolution apologized "to Native Hawaiians on behalf of the people of the United States for the overthrow of the Kingdom of Hawaii on January 17, 1893... and the deprivation of the rights of Native Hawaiians to self-determination."

Since these spiritual practices and traditions from the year 1819 to the early 1970s, have little oral tradition and no written record, I felt it would be valuable to include what was transpiring in Hawai'i during those years, as they are also in large part - what shaped Hawai'i's future going forward from 1819 into present day Hawai'i.

So for those who have only a keen spiritual interest, again, jump to The Awakening... Into the Now! chapter.

For those who desire a more complete picture of the challenges and forces that formed and molded a big part of Hawaiian history – within the over all context of how it affected Hawaiian spiritual practices and traditions - please continue with the next chapter.

10

1778 – 1874
Challenge, Great Adversity, and Adaptation

Captain Cook arrived in 1778. For several centuries before then, and several decades afterward, the ancient Hawaiian religion (as practiced by the second wave of migrations – the time of Pa'ao onwards) was an intimate part of daily life.

Prayers were offered throughout the day to the four major gods and thousands of lesser gods by both ali'i (chiefs) and maka'ainana (commoners) as they went about their ordinary activities such as making important decisions, planning a battle, planting or harvesting, fishing, etc.

Heiaus (stone temples) were constructed in every valley and dedicated to the gods of agriculture (including fishing), the gods of war, or other gods (such as Laka the goddess of hula).

On important occasions human sacrifices were offered to the gods to ensure bountiful crops or success in battle; or during ceremonies to dedicate a new heiau.

Kamehameha The Great received a prophecy that if he would build a large heiau at Kawaihae (northwest corner of Hawaii Island) he would become Hawai'i's greatest conqueror and unify all the islands.

There were hundreds of laws prohibiting various behaviors. Violating any such kapu (taboo) carried a penalty of death unless the perpetrator could flee to a pu'uhonua (a sacred place, or person, of refuge) to do penance and be absolved by a priest.

Many of the taboos seem trivial to today's people - we have difficulty understanding why violating them warranted the death penalty. The explanation lies in the religious beliefs themselves.

For example, stepping on the shadow of a chief or touching a piece of his clothing was thought to weaken the chief's mana (spiritual power).

The chiefs were directly descended from the gods and served as intermediaries among the gods, the land, and the people. The chiefs were responsible for maintaining pono - the proper balance.

Thus any interference with the mana of a chief upset the balance and could result in famine, earthquakes, disease, hurricanes, etc. This was considered true of any offence, that the gods would be displeased and therefore, some form of cataclysm would occur.

Another example is the taboo against women eating specific foods (bananas, coconuts, pigs) which were the embodiments of the gods of masculinity and virility.

And the taboo mentioned in the last chapter – the taboo against men and women eating together on the same mat or at the same table.

When the kapu system was overthrown this severely and devastatingly, changed the Hawaiian's culture and traditions.

It shook and collapsed all of the social foundations and the revered religious premises forever, bringing all social, religious and cultural understandings, not only to standstill, but to an utter and ruinous stop.

Without religion, no social mores, and no sense of guidance or direction, a monumental and traumatic void was created.

Up until the overthrow of the kapu system, everything was held in check, with known laws and rituals. Once the kapu system was no more, everything was in chaos, and confusion.

A large part of this was due to the increased and looming changes as result of the dramatic impact, and widespread influences of endless foreign newcomers.

First, the missionaries arrived only 5 months after the kapu system was overthrown. With the ancient religion already out of the way, they readily sought to grab their opportunity to take charge and begin their monumental task:

"to open our hearts wide and set our mark high. To aim at nothing short of covering these islands with fruitful fields and pleasant dwellings and schools and churches and of *raising up the whole people to an elevated state of Christian civilization."*

The beginning of this tension was foretold and revealed in the last line of paragraph, *raising up the whole people to an elevated state of Christian civilization."*

If they were to raise and elevate the whole people - then their perspective from the start - was that the Hawaiian people and its culture was both of a lower standing and inferior. That in fact, they had come to convert the heathens.

Kamehameha II did not welcome the missionaries with open arms. They were therefore limited to a probationary one-year period to begin with.

Once they were allowed to begin their ministry, they mobilized quickly with mission stations on Oahu and Hawai'i island.

Intrigued and repelled by traditional native customs, the missionaries quickly set about to covert and "civilize" the Hawaiians.

This involved imposition of a strict culture common to the New England ministers whose religion was "intolerant of religious and moral beliefs that were not in accord with their own."

Seeing only a value in their own religious beliefs, they would not and/or could not - see the depth and value of the universal and true ancient Hawaiian Spirituality.

Hawaiian Spirituality and its practices, which included hula as well as all kahuna practices became illegal under the rulership of Kamehameha III, due to the missionaries strong influence.

Wary at first of the new religion, a number of the natives were won over following the conversion of several high-ranking women, including Keopuolani and Kapiolani, both highly respected queens at one point, and Ka'ahumanu, the most powerful woman in all of Hawai'i at the time.

The support of these women was crucial to the missionaries' success, because they were extremely influential. Keopuolani, who was the first convert in 1823, was the highest-born woman in the land and mother of Kamehameha II and Kamehameha III.

Ka'ahumanu served as regent of the kingdom with power almost equal to that of the king. After her conversion, Ka'ahumanu worked zealously for the missionary cause.

Also, because traditionally there had been no division between religion and government, Ka'ahumanu's acceptance of the new religion gave it official sanction in the minds of the people.

Before long, churches were erected, and the native people, used to instruction from religious leaders, became active churchgoers.

Even with the many unprecedented and rapid new changes coming to the islands, many Hawaiians remained firm and steadfast in their ancient spirituality, taking it out of public view and securely underground. By keeping it hidden, they were able to perpetuate their spirituality and keep the flame of spirit alive.

Another new element was added that fueled the social, cultural, and economic turmoil in the islands - the whalers.

They began to arrive in increasing numbers looking for supplies, fuel, food, and water. This onslaught greatly increased demands for goods and services, a situation that commercial interests and foreign governments (largely British and American) were quick to capitalize upon.

The missionary activity - expansionist ambitions, and commercial interests - prevalent in the Hawaiian Islands in the early 1820s set the stage for a battle for control of the Hawaiian kingdom, a battle dominated for the first few decades by the American missionaries.

They would influence Hawaiian politics, foreign relations, and economics for the next half century.

Kamehameha II was ill-equipped to deal with these opposing forces. He was forced to make choices to placate the missionaries while also accommodating the traders and merchants.

Unfortunately, he dismissed many of his father's shrewdest advisors, depending instead upon foreign companions. Heavy drinking clouded many of his decisions.

When he died in London in 1824, he left a troubled monarchy struggling to deal with the changes that had swept throughout the islands.

Between 1825 and 1840, changes in the Hawaiian government were largely influenced by foreign ideas and the American missionaries.

Conversion of Hawaiians such as Keopuolani and Ka'ahumanu to Christianity swiftly paved the way for far reaching and desperate changes in the culture and traditions of all Hawaiians.

For example, Ka'ahumanu, once the favorite wife of Kamehameha, possessed more power and property than any other Hawaiian woman.

Following her conversion to Christianity, she rigidly enforced many of the religious dictates of the missionaries among her people. During the 1820s, these dictates were established as laws, enforced by the missionaries but resisted strongly by the foreign traders and merchants.

Following Ka'ahumamu's death, Hawaiian leaders attempted unsuccessfully to regain native Hawaiian control of the islands and return to the old ways. Foreigners, especially the American missionaries, continued to influence the Hawaiian government.

By the 1830s there was a growing sentiment among the Hawaiians for more self determination. After two decades of Christian instruction, Hawaiian leaders "were forced to consider in earnest a fundamental reconstruction of the government of the kingdom of Hawai'i."

As the numbers of influential foreigners in the community continued to increase, so did questions as to their rights to property and a place in the community.

Imperialistic pressures from various foreign nations began to raise the question of independence.

Two of the most important changes were the development of the Hawaiian Constitution, and a revision of the Hawaiian land tenure system.

Foreigners using or holding Hawaiian lands were very anxious to secure title to them. Resident merchants saw future opportunities for large-scale agriculture and capital investments and viewed the land tenure system as a roadblock to progress.

Unfortunately, the constitution (which was intended to help native Hawaiians) and the 1850 land law were all too often manipulated to the advantage of the fiercely competitive foreign business and commercial interests and land-hungry foreigners.

On top of all this, the Hawaiian population which was estimated to be between 400,000 to one million inhabitants pre-contact, was decimated by contagious diseases such as cholera, measles, chicken pox, influenza, and syphilis, brought in by the foreigners, for which the immune systems and medical experts of the natives, were completely unprepared.

By 1953 the Hawaiian population had dwindled down to 71,019 people. It has been estimated as low as 40,000 by 1890.

11

King David Kalākaua
A Breath of Life to the Hawaiian Spirit

Through all of the adversity and adaptation it was King David Kalākaua in 1874, that brought a breath of life back to the Hawaiian Spirit.

At the time he was elected, foreigners dominated the Hawaiian government. Realizing that the influence and powers of the missionaries and foreigners were positioned to take over and control the little remaining Hawaiian authority, Kalākaua quickly moved to make the needed changes to give "Hawai'i back to the Hawaiians."

Kalākaua promised to put native Hawaiians back into the Kingdom's government. He also promised to amend the Kingdom's constitution.

King Kalākaua believed in the hereditary right of the ali'i to rule. During the early part of Kalākaua's reign, the king made full use of his power to appoint and dismiss cabinets. Kalākaua continually dismissed cabinets and appointed new ones, aimed at improving the needs and benefits of the Hawaiian people.

To best engage and inspire his people, Kalākaua began his reign with a tour of the Hawaiian islands. This increased his popularity and gained favor and loyalty.

Then in November 1875, Kalākaua traveled to Washington, D.C to meet President Ulysses S. Grant, to negotiate a reciprocity treaty to help end a depression that was ongoing in Hawai'i. An agreement was reached and the treaty was signed on January 30, 1875.

The treaty allowed certain Hawaiian goods, mainly sugar and rice, to be admitted into the United States tax-free.

In 1881, King Kalākaua left Hawai'i on a trip around the world. During this trip, he met with many Presidents, Queens, Emperors and other crowned heads of state. In this, he became the first king to travel around the world.

Kalākaua continually took steps to perpetuate nationalism. Kalākaua replaced the considerably Christian national anthem He Mele Lahui Hawai'i with Hawai'i Ponoī in 1876, a song inspired by Kamehameha I.

The overall intention was to form a contemporary national identity rather than modeling Hawai'i after Great Britain and/or the culture of the United States.

Along with this Kalākaua dreamed of a royal palace befitting of the sovereignty of a modern state such as Hawai'i. He had 'Iolani Palace built as the fulfillment of this vision.

'Iolani Palace the only royal palace that exists on American soil today, was built at a cost of over $300,000 – a sum unheard of at the time. Many of the furnishings in the palace were ordered by Kalākaua while he was in Europe.

Despite early efforts to earn favor with the missionaries and the foreigner's growing powers, he began putting the needs of his people first. The Hawaiian people loved him; however, the missionaries did not enjoy their dealings with Kalākaua.

The missionaries descendants had gained power in Hawai'i by buying land. They were so high in dealings with the island's inner workings that they had to meet with Kalākaua, as advisors almost, only Kalākaua didn't always agree with their opinions.

He always put his people first, and that meant most times denying the missionaries and foreigner's requests and ideas.

Kalākaua spent three years planning his second coronation in 1883 to try and ease the racial tensions between the local people and the missionaries descendants and foreigners, with 8,000 people attending.

Kalākaua sponsored several traditional Hawaiian practices such as hula, chanting, sports, and royal rituals. He also had Hawaiian myths, legends, and chants recorded in media.

By 1887, the Missionary party had grown very frustrated with Kalākaua. They blamed him for the Kingdom's growing debt and accused him of being a spendthrift.

Some foreigners wanted to force King Kalākaua to abdicate and put his sister Lili'uokalani onto the throne, while others wanted to end the monarchy altogether and annex the islands to the United States.

The people who favored annexation formed a group called the Hawaiian League. In 1887, members of the League armed with guns assembled together. The members of the league forced King Kalākaua at gun point to sign a new constitution.

This new constitution, nicknamed the Bayonet Constitution of 1887, removed much of the King's executive power and deprived most native Hawaiians of their voting rights. 75% of ethnic Hawaiians could not vote at all, because of the new gender, literacy, property, and age requirements.

Moreover, the legislature was now able to override a veto by the King, and the King was no longer allowed to take action without approval of the cabinet. The House of Nobles, the house of legislature appointed by the King, were to be elected.

King Kalākaua earned the nickname "the Merrie Monarch," because of his love of the joyful elements of life.

During his reign, **hula** and **chanting** were revived, after having been banned in 1830. Today, his name lives on in the Merrie Monarch Festival, an internationally celebrated hula festival named in his honor. He is also known to have revived the

Hawaiian martial art, Lua as well as surfing.

He wrote **Hawai'i Pono'ī**, which is the state song of Hawaii today. King Kalākaua's ardent support of the then newly introduced **ukulele** as a Hawaiian instrument led to its becoming symbolic of Hawaii and Hawaiian culture.

By 1890, King Kalākaua's health began to fail. Under the advice of his physician, he traveled to San Francisco for treatment. His health continued to worsen, and he died on January 20, 1891 at the Palace Hotel in San Francisco. His remains were returned to Honolulu.

Because he and his wife, Queen Kapi'olani did not have any children, Kalākaua's sister, Lili'uokalani, succeeded him to the Hawaiian throne.

12

Queen Lili'uokalani
& the Overthrow
of the Hawaiian Kingdom

By the time Queen Lili'uokalani inherited the throne (January 29, 1891) from her brother, King David Kalākaua, the corrupt influences and foreign powers had all but taken over the rule of Hawai'i.

In response to this, Queen Lili'uokalani immediately set about drastically changing the present (bayonet) constitution, to give the power back to the Hawaiian government and the Hawaiian people.

She drafted a new constitution that would restore the veto power to the monarchy and voting rights to economically disenfranchised native Hawaiians.

The effort to draft a new constitution never came to fruition, and it preceded the U.S. invasion, occupation and overthrow of the Hawaiian Kingdom government.

Threatened by the queen's proposed new constitution, American and European businessmen and residents organized to depose Queen Lili'uokalani, asserting that the queen had "virtually abdicated" by refusing to support the 1887 Constitution.

Business interests within the Kingdom were also upset about what they viewed as "poor governance" of the Kingdom, as well as the U.S. removal of foreign tariffs in the sugar trade due to the McKinley Tariff.

The tariff eliminated the favored status of Hawaiian sugar guaranteed by the Reciprocity Treaty of 1875. Americans and Europeans actively sought the Hawaiian Kingdom's annexation to the United States.

This was largely brought about by the children of the missionaries (now adults) who through the years had garnered large plots of land to grow agricultural products and who made hugh profits, primarily through sugar cane and pineapple.

As the tension and fight for power increased over who owned the land, who had certain rights, and who held the power to rule over the Hawaiian Kingdom, it now all came to a head, as a result of the children of the missionaries selfish commercial interests.

As the coup d'état was unfolding, the Committee of Safety (a foreign organization made up mostly of Americans) expressed concern for the safety and property of American citizens.

In response, United States Government Minister John L Stevens summoned a company of US Marines from the USS Boston and two companies of U.S. Navy sailors to take up positions at the U.S. Legation, Consulate, and Arion Hall.

On the afternoon of January 16, 1893, 162 sailors and U.S. Marines aboard the USS Boston in Honolulu Harbor came ashore under orders of neutrality.

Historian William Russ has noted that the presence of these troops, ostensibly to enforce neutrality and prevent violence, effectively made it impossible for the monarchy to protect itself.

The actual overthrow was surprisingly smooth. Under orders of the queen, half a dozen policemen were sent to I'olani palace to arrest any members from the Committee of Safety who tried to enter the palace.

After a shooting broke out close to the palace, some policemen went to the scene. One of the policemen was shot, and had to be carried by the remaining palace guards.

This left the palace open to the Committee of Safety. With almost no audience except for some government clerks, the Committee of Safety signed a document that ended the Hawaiian monarchy. Lili'uokalani would not find out until the next day.

The Queen was deposed on January 17, 1893, and temporarily relinquished her throne to "the superior military forces of the United States". She had signed in the hope that the United States, would soon restore Hawaii's sovereignty to the rightful holder.

Queen Lili'uokalani issued the following statement yielding her authority to the United States Government rather than to the Provisional

Government:

I, Lili'uokalani, by the Grace of God and under the constitution of the Hawaiian Kingdom, Queen, do hereby solemnly protest against any and all acts done against myself and the constitutional government of the Hawaiian Kingdom by certain persons claiming to have established a Provisional Government of and for this Kingdom.

That I yield to the superior force of the United States of America, whose Minister Plenipotentiary, His Excellency John L Stevens, has caused United States troops to be landed at Honolulu and declared that he would support the said Provisional Government.

Now, to avoid any collision of armed forces and perhaps loss of life, I do, under this protest, and impelled by said forces, yield my authority until such time as the Government of the United States shall, upon the facts being presented to it, undo the action of its representative and reinstate me in the authority which I claim as the constitutional sovereign of the Hawaiian Islands.

— Queen Lili'uokalani, Jan 17, 1893

A provisional government, composed of European and American businessmen, was then instituted until annexation with the United States could be achieved.

On February 1, 1893, the US Minister (ambassador) to Hawaii proclaimed Hawaii a protectorate of the United States.

In 1898, Hawai'i became an incorporated territory of the United States. In 1900, the US Congress passed the Hawai'i Organic Act establishing a government for the Territory of Hawai'i.

Upon her death, Lili'uokalani dictated in her will that all of her possessions and properties be sold and the money raised would go to the Queen Lili'uokalani Children's Trust to help orphaned and indigent children. The Queen Lili'uokalani Trust Fund still exists today.

13
1900 - 1959
The Territory Years of Hawai'i

Sugar plantations in Hawai'i expanded during the territorial period. Some of the companies diversified and came to dominate related industries including transportation, banking and real estate. Economic and political power was concentrated in large corporations.

Attack on Pearl Harbor

Pearl Harbor was attacked on 7 December 1941 by Japan, triggering the United States' entry into World War II. Most Americans had never heard of Pearl Harbor, even though it had been used by the US Navy since the Spanish American War. Hawaii was put under martial law until the end of the war.

The Democratic Party

In 1954 a nonviolent revolution of industry-wide strikes, protests, and other civil disobedience transpired. In the territorial elections of 1954 the reign of the Hawaii Republican Party in the legislature came to an abrupt end, replaced by the Democratic Party of Hawai'i.

Democrats lobbied for statehood and gained the governorship from 1962 to 2002. The Revolution also unionized the labor force, hastening the decline of the plantations.

Statehood

All islands voted at least 93% in favor of statehood in 1959. President Dwight D. Eisenhower signed the Hawaii Admission Act on March 18, 1959 which allowed for Hawaiian statehood. Hawaii was admitted as the 50th state on August 21, 1959.

Hawaiian Sovereignty movements

For many Native Hawaiians, the manner in which Hawai'i became a US territory is a bitter part of its history. Hawaii Territory governors and judges were direct political appointees of the US president.

Native Hawaiians created the Home Rule Party for greater self-government. Hawaii was subject to cultural and societal repression during the territorial period and the first decade of statehood.

Along with other self-determination movements worldwide during the 1960s & 1970s, the Hawaiian Renaissance led to the rebirth of Hawaiian language, culture and identity.

With the support of Hawaii Senators Daniel Inouye

and Daniel Akaka, Congress passed a joint resolution called the "Apology Resolution" (US Public Law 103-150.)

It was signed by President Bill Clinton on November 23, 1993. This resolution apologized "to Native Hawaiians on behalf of the people of the United States for the overthrow of the Kingdom of Hawaii on January 17, 1893... and the deprivation of the rights of Native Hawaiians to self-determination." The implications of this resolution have been extensively debated.

14
The Hawaiian Renaissance

Given all the unimaginable and drastic changes to the Hawaiian ancient traditions and culture since 1819, it is of paramount value to share the immense importance the Hawaiian renaissance has played on the resurgence of the Hawaiian culture, its people and it's spirit.

I have found no better way to share this, nor could I find the words myself, to express it, as it has been conveyed so eloquently and ardently by George Hu'eu Kanahele (1930 - 2000.)

George was a native Hawaiian, an activist, historian and author.

This talk was given in May, 1979

"Let me say, first of all, we're not really here to listen to me talk about the Hawaiian Renaissance - we're here to celebrate it. For if anything is worth celebrating, it is that we are still alive, that our culture has survived the onslaughts of change during the past 200 years. Indeed, not only has it survived, it is now thriving.

Look at the thousands of young men dancing the hula; or the overflow Hawaiian language classes at the university; or the revived Hawaiian music industry; or the astounding productivity of Hawaiian craftsmen and artists.

Consider such unprecedented events as the voyage of the Hokule'a, the occupation of Kaho'olawe, and passage of the Hawaiian package at the Constitutional Convention.

Like a dormant volcano coming to life again, the Hawaiians are erupting with all the pent-up energy and frustrations of people on the make. This great happening has been called a "psychological renewal," a "reaffirmation," a "revival" or "resurgence" and a "renaissance."

No matter what you call it, it is the most significant chapter in 20th century Hawaiian history.

Why? Because it has reversed years of cultural decline; it has created a new kind of Hawaiian consciousness; it has inspired greater pride in being Hawaiian;

it has led to bold and imaginative ways of reasserting our identity; it has led to a new political awareness; and it has had and will continue to have a positive impact on the economic and social uplifting of the Hawaiian community.

How did it come about? What is its shape and magnitude? How does it compare with eras of the past? What does it mean for Hawaiians? And non-Hawaiians? And what about its future? These are some of the questions we need to have answered.

The renaissance encompasses more than the creation of works of art and literature. It also includes a revival of interest in the past, in the pursuit of knowledge or learning and in the future.

In short, it deals with the revitalization of the human spirit in all aspects of endeavor. *And when we look very carefully at what is occurring among Hawaiians today economically, artistically, politically, socially, culturally, it is impossible to ignore the spirit of rebirth. I think the word "renaissance" fits.*

The King David Kalākaua renaissance was short lived, for after he died, it was just four years before the Hawaiian Kingdom came to an end.

The collapse of national sovereignty had an almost fatal effect on Hawaiian cultural integrity. I cannot say how much was lost as a result, for this is a subject that needs a great deal more research and reflection, but it must have been enormous.

It is not until the 1920s that we see a resurgence of Hawaiian activity but of a socio-cultural and political nature.

This was the movement led by Prince Jonah Kuhio aimed at rehabilitating Hawaiians through a homesteading scheme, and returning them to the land.

As a compliment to this program, he also established the Hawaiian Civic Club designed to promote the educational and cultural welfare of native Hawaiians.

The results of Kuhio's efforts were, at best, uneven

and represent something less than a renaissance.

There have been other individuals who have attempted to stir up interest in preserving and maintaining Hawaiian traditions and arts.

In the 1930s, George Mossman, the charismatic founder of Lalani Village, tried almost single handedly to regenerate public interest in Hawaiiana, particularly the language, chant and hula.

His village, consisting of traditional Hawaiian grass huts and even a heiau, all of which he built himself, was probably the first "Hawaiian cultural center." He offered classes in language, chant, hula, crafts and some of the ancient rituals

Another individual initiative emerged in the 1950s when Malia Solomon developed her famous Ulu Mau Village, somewhat in the spirit and style of Lalani Village.

Her interest and skills were in crafts such as tapa-making and weaving, and consequently she emphasized aspects of the culture that others had not.

But Ulu Mau Village eventually faded away, not for lack of inspired leadership and commitment on the part of Malia, but for lack of a responsive public.

Soon however, the mainland would be in the throes of the black civil rights movement. With its demands for equality and self-determination, the movement inspired other minorities to press their grievances.

The fight for civil rights ushered in the "Age of Ethnicity" whose main credo was that there was nothing wrong in maintaining one's ethnic identity.

The time period also engendered a spirit of defiance and rebelliousness that was reflected in the great counter-culture of the '50s, rock 'n roll.

Elvis, the Beatles, long hair, new clothes styles, drugs - in a way these were but expressions of independence against the established order. A new generation had arrived to create its own world.

Vietnam was an important part of this period, nourishing the nation-wide mood of questioning of authority and old myths through protests, demonstrations, draft-card burning, desertions and escapes to Sweden and Canada by young men who believed the war was wrong.

So this spirit of protest and all the values and activities it engendered, had an impact on American ethnic groups such as the Chicanos and Puerto Ricans - and the Hawaiians.

It's impossible to measure it, but its effects were observable or at least felt in the 1960s when Hawaiians, as individuals and groups, showed an increasing concern for their political rights and grievances and their cultural identity.

The seminal statement of this period was, perhaps, John Dominis Holt's "On Being Hawaiian" an emotional but powerful reaffirmation of the

Hawaiian and his place in society. It was published in 1964.

A rather significant event - looking back now because it wasn't considered so then - was probably the establishment of the State Council on Hawaiian Heritage because it was the first time the State of Hawaii officially recognized the value of perpetuating the culture in this manner. This was done in 1969.

There were other Hawaiian cultural happening such as the growth in the popularity of Hawaiian canoe paddling, the emerging comeback of the male hula, the formation of Hui Kukekuka and Hui Na Opio and similar cultural groups, all by the late 1960s.

And finally, the first political demonstrations that began with Kalama Valley in early 1970 when protesters sought to prevent Bishop Estate from ousting a pig farmer.

It was not until the early 1970s that the Hawaiian Renaissance really flowered and attained the influence it has today.

So you can see that the events of this decade are the logical culmination of events and causes that happened before, including the efforts of many individuals and groups, such as King David Kalākaua, Prince Jonah Kuhio, George Mossman, Malia Solomon and many others.

History, after all, is a continuum with its own karma. but what makes the '70s different from any of these past events and efforts is the sheer size, intensity and numbers of people involved in the Renaissance.

The Renaissance can best be understood in terms of before and after, comparing the level of activity on or prior to 1970 and now. Take Hawaiian music as an example.

In January, 1971, I wrote in the Honolulu Advertiser that "Hawaiian music was in its death throes." there was only a handful of steel guitar players, all of whom were aging; young people were turned on to rock 'n roll and could care less for Hawaiian music; only one radio station in Honolulu bothered to play it regularly;

slack key guitar music was almost unheard of; there was only one hotel featuring a Hawaiian show; and outside Hawai'i Hawaiian music, once so popular throughout the world, was all but dead.

Today, the resurgence of Hawaiian music is one of the strongest evidences for the Renaissance. Young people are now turned on to Hawaiian music as they had once been turned on to rock earlier.

The Cazimero Brothers, Gabby Pahinui, Olomana, and the Sons of Hawai'i are as familiar to them as The Village People and Peter Frampton. There appears to be more young - and old - people learning to play Hawaiian music, more teaching and more performing it, than at any time in the past 20 - 30 years.

For the first time in modern Hawaiian history, we have an organization set up to perpetuate Hawaiian music, the Hawaiian Music Foundation.

Set up in Feb. 1971, it is the first of what I call the Renaissance organizations. In 1972, it held the first slack key guitar concert, and in 1973, the first falsetto and steel guitar concerts.

Significantly, the impetus for the resurgence in Hawaiian music has come almost entirely, if not entirely, from the local community. It has not come from the outside nor from the tourism industry.

You can tell by the songs: the lyrics are in Hawaiian, the themes are Hawaiian, the composers, for the most part, are Hawaiian. And what can be more Hawaiian than the chant which has been a vital part of the current revival in Hawaiian music?

One of the more exciting aspects of the Renaissance is the revival of the hula kahiko and male hula. Nobody can help but be impressed with the dancers and performances today of the ancient hula, but it was not too long ago that Mary Kawena Pukui predicted that by now there would be no more hula.

It was in 1946 that she stated, as quoted in the Honolulu Advertiser, that the "real hula was dying out, and that there were only about a dozen Hawaiians who could dance the hula as it should be danced according to the old Hawaiian custom. She predicted that within 320 years the tradition will have vanished into the realm of memory."

Well, I think in this instance she would gladly

recant, because she has played a part in keeping the tradition alive.

So have many others from Ilalaole to Akoni and Ha'aheo, from Lokalia Montgomery and Iolani to Kaui Zuttemeister and Edith Kanakaole.

But, most important to the Renaissance is the cadre of young kumu hula who have taught hundreds and who will yet teach hundreds more in the years to come.

While I don't have any comparative figures, I am prepared to wager that there are more young people learning and dancing the ancient hula in the '70s than during any other decade of this century.

The evidence may be gleaned form the number of participants in the Merry Monarch Festival, the King Kamehameha Celebration hula competitions, and other contests.

In fact, there are more hula competitions today than at any other time in recent memory. If you need more evidence, look at the figures of the attendance at the annual dance conferences of the State Council on Hawaiian Heritage. In ten years they have increased nearly a thousand-fold.

It is important to note that today's interest is greater for the ancient than the modern hula. The more traditional the dance, the keener, the interest. It's as if people want to get as close as they possibly can to the first hula that the Kanaka did.

While dance and music enjoy the highest visibility,

there has been great interest shown in other arts and crafts of Hawai'i-nei.

Take, for example, featherwork, which the ancient Hawaiian craftsmen did more skillfully and beautifully than any other Polynesians.

40 years ago it was virtually extinct except for a few practitioners such as Johanna Cluney. But in recent years several thousand people have taken up the lost art.

Another example in the art field is the dramatic emergence of another Renaissance organization, Hale Nauä III, made up of Hawaiian artists.

Set up in 1976, they have already made an impression on the community through their exhibits culminating in their recent Bishop Museum show.

Since it was the first time in the 90-year old museum's history that a contemporary exhibit was allowed in its halls, it means something.

I don't know exactly what, from the museum's point of view at least, but I think it has given credence to the Society's claims that they are Hawaiian artists who produce Hawaiian art imbued with a Hawaiian feeling.

Although one can certainly argue this point - after all, the world view of the ancient Hawaiian artists was much different from contemporary Hawaiian artists, no matter what we may say - what's important is their belief that their art is an expression of their Hawaiian identity.

Another manifestation of the Renaissance is in sports, which was such a huge part of the life of ancient Hawaiians. We all know what has happened to the sport of Hawai'i's kings - surfing.

It was nearly dead by the turn of the century but by the 1960s surfing had not only become the number one water sport in Hawai'i, but had also become an international craze.

Incidentally, next to Hawaiian music, surfing is the only other aspect of Hawaiian culture that has been so widely accepted around the world.

[Canoe paddling is yet another manifestation of the Renaissance.] Of course, one canoe stands alone, the Hokule'a.

Its successful voyage to Tahiti and back is one of the most singular achievements to happen during the Hawaiian Renaissance because it symbolized one of the greatest accomplishments of the Polynesians. It was an extraordinary feat by any definition.

One of the most fundamental givens of a culture is its language, and no culture can long survive, let alone achieve a renaissance, without its language being spoken and understood.

I can remember when people said and when I said it, too, the Hawaiian language is dying. We know its' been dying for a long time.

When Kaunamano established his Hawaiian language newspaper in 1861 - the first native

Hawaiian to do so - he was afraid it was dying too.

And only last year, Leslie Kuloloio of Wailuku, Maui told a congressional hearing that the Hawaiian language is an "endangered species," when less than 1 percent of the state's estimated 30,000 Hawaiian children are able to speak it.

But isn't it reassuring to know that the University of Hawai'i has so many students wishing to register for Hawaiian classes that neither its staff nor budget can cope with the demand?

Characteristically, as in music, art and other fields, persons interested in keeping Hawaiian values alive organized themselves.

So in 1972, another Renaissance organization, Aha Hui Olelo Hawai'i, was born. It has grown in numbers and activities. One of its most interesting is the weekly talks now on KCCN conducted entirely in Hawaiian.

Isn't it heartening to know that high schools, both private and public, teach Hawaiian? The classes at Kailua High have been so popular that one teacher has barely been able to handle the load.

Kamehameha, of course, has been offering Hawaiian for several years, although it has had a rather spotty record in this regard.

Can you imagine that at one time Kamehameha proscribed its teaching and even punished students who were caught speaking Hawaiian.

Isn't it good to know that after many years of

campaigning that the Department of Education has allowed Hawaiian to be taught at the elementary school level in communities where there are large numbers of Hawaiian pupils?

You know that not only Hawaiians but non-ethnic Hawaiians as well have long taken an interest in learning and maintaining the language.

In fact, some of our best teachers, as well as speakers, have not a drop of Hawaiian blood.

One of the distinguishing characteristics of the Renaissance is a great interest in studying the past and in the pursuit of knowledge in general. There is no mistaking that this is also true of the Hawaiian Renaissance.

From young composers to canoe paddlers, from ethnomusicologists to artist, from students to professors, there's a kind of stampede back to the past. Everybody seems to be shouting, "Ho'i ana i ke kumu" or Back to the source."

In our reflecting on our past, I think we should remind ourselves of the important place that the intellectuals occupied in the Hawaiian elite. They were, after all, the kahunas, the scholar-priests, or at least some of them were.

Since there was no written language everything had to be recorded in the memory banks of these intellectual giants. The old Hawaiians, therefore, must have had enormous respect for the human mind and for those who were gifted in its use. How good it is to see us rediscovering this traditional value.

Having made the case for the Hawaiian Renaissance, let me now try to draw some meaning for you and the people of Hawai'i.

First, as human beings and, of course, as Hawaiians, we should all be elated that a once rich culture threatened with extinction has been able to survive and now appears to be thriving in spite of the odds against it.

The Renaissance does not mean a literal rebirth of classical Hawaiian traditions, dances, chants and so forth. To believe otherwise is to make a fetish out of tradition.

Creative artists are not mindless copycats. They strive to express their own selves and their own time. They are different, but yet they still retain some identifiable characteristics that we can call Hawaiian.

What precisely are those characteristics, those standards by which we judge what is artistically and culturally honest, are sometimes questionable.

Sometimes they lead to arguments. And, God knows, we have a lot of arguments among Hawaiians. Maybe that, too, is evidence of dynamic culture. I don't know.

At any rate, while we try to insist on certain standards of cultural integrity and authenticity, we must realize the historical reality of inevitable change.

Thus, in our efforts to rediscover our roots, to reaffirm our heritage, to revive our past, we cannot always be too clear about precisely what we are rediscovering, reaffirming, or reviving.

It may well be that much, if not most, of what we are reviving is new traditions that look like old traditions.

Has the Renaissance influenced the political thinking and behavior of Hawaiians? No question. Kaho'olawe couldn't have happened in the 1950s or even the 1960s.

The Renaissance was the incubator for a lot of the sympathetic feelings that the issue received from among Hawaiians, especially young Hawaiians, and non-Hawaiians alike.

The protest songs written by young composers for Kaho'olawe were part and parcel of the resurgence of Hawaiian music.

The rhetoric of aloha aina symbolized the whole movement of going back to the source, listening to our kupuna, finding our roots.

Finally, there is a paradox about the Renaissance we need to understand. It is that the Renaissance does not only belong to Hawaiians. It belongs to non-ethnic Hawaiians, too.

Could you exclude, for example a Donald Mitchell, a Jack Waterhouse, a Peter Moon, a Keola Cabacungan, a Rev. Harada, or a Dorothy Hazama just because by some genetic accident they don't happen to be Hawaiian?

Would you exclude a Pat Bacon, the hanai daughter of Kawena Pukui, who is fluent in Hawaiian, who is a master teacher of the hula and a chanter, just because she is pure Japanese?

The plain fact is that historically non-Hawaiians have always played a large role in preserving and perpetuaing Hawaiian culture and its ideals.

The Rev. Lorenzo Lyons, "Makua Laiana," the composer of Hawai'i Aloha. Henry Berger, who preserved and changed Hawaiian music; Alexander Hume Ford, who helped revive surfing and canoe paddling at the turn of the century; Prof. Kuykendall, whose history of Hawai'i remains the classic reference work; Dr. Peter Buck and Kenneth Emory and...the list goes on and on.

Today there are probably as many non-ethnic Hawaiians as there are Hawaiians actively engaged in the Renaissance:

haoles, Japanese, Chinese, Filipinos, etc. people who have no Hawaiian ancestry but who for one reason or another have come to identify themselves culturally, psychologically and spiritually with Hawaiianness.

These Hawaiians-at-heart have key positions in many Hawaiian causes, and often it has been their support in money, time and counsel that has spelled the difference between success and failure.

Unfortunately, but true, some Hawaiians choose to ignore this fact. They are so self-conscious about their new-found Hawaiianness that they become suspicious of every haole or Oriental who may want to help.

Some insist on excluding non-Hawaiians from any Hawaiian-related activity, purely on the basis or race - a case of reverse racism.

What the Renaissance confirms to me is that a lot of people in Hawai'i care deeply about what is happening to those values and customs that make Hawai'i, unique and special.

Anybody who claims or wants Hawai'i to be home, in some degree or another, wants and, even needs to share in its Hawaiianness.

The beautiful thing about the Renaissance is that it offers Hawaiians the greatest opportunity we have had since Kamehameha I to unify the people of these islands not by the power of the sword but by the influence of our ideals, or values and our aloha."

While this is the most pertinent part of what George Kanahele shared (in terms of what this book is about) the complete version of his talk can be found online via google, type in **The Hawaiian Renaissance by George S. Kanahele May 1979.**

15

The Awakening...
Into the Now!

Today, many hear the call to Hawai'i.
More and more are arriving. Many share there is something here for them, though most can't put it into words... a feeling, a vibration, a knowing, they say.

People come from all around the world, and they are deeply touched by their experiences here. Some say it feels more like home, than any other place they have been too or have ever lived.

The Aloha Spirit reigns supreme here in Hawai'i and those who have experienced it before are either coming "home," to not only experience and be immersed in it once again, but to help recreate and perpetuate the Aloha Spirit.

And for those not able to move back, they are coming into the awareness that something is shifting on both a deep inner personal level *and* on a global as well.

Souls are recognizing that there is so much more to life than meets the eye. That there is a way of life that can include harmony, balance, creativity, and the Aloha Spirit!

Along with this, there is the recognition and

importance of the ideals of unity, community, awareness, centeredness, absolute love (Aloha Spirit) respect, and love of others, that will bring this way of life into manifestation.

In large part, the Lemurian civilization was created to introduce spirituality into the world.
As mentioned in the Mu chapter, there were 350 million souls, who over the course of twenty thousand years, lived in radiant peace, unconditional love and harmonious cooperation.

As far as is known, this has never been achieved previous to Lemuria, nor has it ever been accomplished since.

Through time the Lemurian souls have all been reincarnated at different times and different places throughout the world - but not as Lemurians.

But they all carry a Lemurian seed within, knowingly or unknowingly, that activates after a predestined timeline, and under certain conditions - and we have crossed that timeline, and those conditions have been meet.

The primary condition was to reach a threshold of spiritual and compassionate awareness on a global, as well as, on a deep inner level.
That threshold was crossed in 2012.

We have moved into 2012 with a new - higher frequency and vibration. Only less than one-half of one percent of seven billion people need awaken to shift the global awareness towards love and compassion.

It's not that many. In fact, it's only 10% of the 350 million Lemurians who are alive today and on the planet today – a very reasonable percentage.

DID YOU CATCH THAT?

Only 10% of the **350 million Lemurians who are alive today! All the souls that once lived in Lemuria during the many thousands of years of Great Peace, Harmony and immersed in the Aloha Spirit, are all on the planet today, at the same time.**

While we have been reincarnated at different times and different places throughout time, we, the Lumerian seed carriers have never all been on the planet at the same time!

This gives us great hope, it is time for monumental celebration, and colossal rejoicing.

The 2012 shift was preceded by the1987 Harmonic Convergence. As well as the completion of the magnetic grid, and the beginning of the crystalline experience in 2002. In 2004, the tsunami and the Venus Transit. And in 2012, another Venus Transit.

These were/are the delivery events of compassionate feminine energy into this world, **to be picked up and used slowly... so you can**

move into the next energy with integrity. These events helped provide a compassionate balance to a planet that has not been balanced for eons.

**What are your dreams?
What is your inspiration?
What kind of world would you
like to live in, to co-create...**

A world full with harmony, cooperation, balance, *and* love (Aloha Spirit!)

A world where everything flows unceasingly in a supportive and helpful manner.

A inspiring world created for your own highest good. Where everything works to inspire you to live your best life possible.

Where people love you, appreciate you, and respect you, and offer comfort and guidance when needed or requested.

A world in which everyone is fully aware that Spirit permeates all life, that Spirit's presence lives and breathes in all things - people, animals, plants, rocks, water, the stars and the heavens. That Spirit's presence is intertwined and radiating within all things.

Imagine every person a valued friend rather than stranger or a potential danger,

a community of people all doing their very best
to add their gift towards everyone's highest
benefit.

A world where laughter and kindness
flow freely and without reservation.

Where much time is put aside for joyous
celebration, merriment, storytelling, spending time
with loved ones and family, all those near and
dear.

Where everything is recognized as a gift from the
Creator, and gratitude for the Creator is abundant
and without end.

And that we are all caretakers of all Spirit
has given us - and we are fully committed to
sharing and protecting the productivity and
fruitfulness of these gifts.

A world of unceasing wonder
and extraordinary beauty.

With what we have within us, and with the
increasing shift of higher awareness and greater
consciousness, we could do exactly that.
Do you accept that?
Then do it.
Do it!

Join the millions of magnificent souls who are
reawaking and remembering and already working,
both individually and together, to create not just a

loose-knit community network of inspired souls, but an extraordinary and beautiful world... created on the foundations and ideals of living in harmony, unity, cooperation, balance, and gratitude - based in the Aloha Spirit!

16

To Enhance, Enrich and Deepen...

Offered here are several authentic Hawaiian methods to enhance, enrich, and deepen, **your spiritual life** and **your overall life experiences**.

They will help you gain a sense of deep calmness and inner peace, radiant well-being, deep relaxation, expanded awareness, and intuitive wisdom.

These meditaions were practiced by Kahuna of ancient times.

You may practice them at any time, but if practiced them at 6 am, noon, 6 pm, or midnight, you will more easily be able to meditate and meditate more deeply.

Also, just when you rise in the morning, or just before you go to bed at night - will prove to be excellent times as well.

The "Aloha" Meditation

This meditation is quite easy.
To begin: Simply sit comfortably, with your back (spine) straight. Close your eyes, while gently turning them upwards towards the point between the eyebrows.

Inhale – mentally count to eight
Hold the breath - mentally count to eight
Exhale - mentally count to eight
Do this 4 times.

With the next inhalation
mentally affirm "Alo"
and with the next exhalation
with a whispered voice
affirm "Ha."

Simply keep mentally repeating "Alo"
with each inhalation
and with whispered voice
"Ha" with each exhalation.

**The inhalation
is through the nose,**

**and your exhalation
is through the mouth**

**with the whispered
sound of "Ha."**

Keep mentally repeating "Alo"
with each inhalation
and with whispered voice "Ha"
with each exhalation.

If your mind wonders,
or becomes distracted,
simply start again with "Alo"
on the next inhalation

and "Ha"
on the next exhalation.

Practice this for 10 minutes
or, as long as you comfortably can.
When you are finished
with the "Alo – Ha"
meditation technique,
continue to sit quietly
and enjoy the stillness
and serenity you feel.

The first sign of a successful "Aloha" meditation is
an uplifted inner feeling of radiant peace.
To fully appeciate the value of the "Aloha"
meditation - one must understand the true depth
of the meaning of Aloha:

"God is Aloha."
*"Aloha is the power of God seeking to unite
what is separated in the world - the power that
unites heart with heart, soul with soul, life with life,
culture with culture, race with race, nation with
nation.*

*Aloha is the power that can reunite when a quarrel
has brought separation; aloha is the power that
reunites a man with himself when he has become
separated from the image of God within."*

~ Rev. Abraham K. Akaka

Each time we do the "Aloha Meditation"

or say, or even think the word "Aloha," we confirm our greater spiritual reality, reignite our innate sense of wholeness and affirm our oneness with the Creator.

A deeper experience of the "Aloha" meditation will invoke a sense of inner clarity, radiant well-being, expanded awareness, and heightened inspiration.

It will confirm our part in the whole, and instill in us gratitude and a reverence for all life.

Please note:
If you cannot sit, if it is not easy to sit comfortably. This meditation can be done with eyes closed, while standing as well.

The "Ha" Meditation
with Piko Piko Breathing

This meditation is quite easy as well.
Begin as with the "Aloha" Meditation:
Simply sit comfortably, with your back (spine) straight. Close your eyes, and gently turn them upwards towards the point between the eyebrows.

Inhale – mentally count to eight
Hold the breath - mentally count to eight
Exhale - mentally count to eight
Do this 4 times.

Now, with the next inhalation
focus your attention

on the crown of your head

and with the next exhalation
focus on your navel area
making the sound of "Ha"
as you release your breath.

Again, focus your attention
on the crown of your head
while inhaling

and focus on your navel area
with the next exhalation
making the sound of "Ha"
as you release your breath.

**The main difference
between the "Ha" Meditation
and the "Aloha" Meditation**

**is that while the inhalation
is still through the nose,**

**and your exhalation
is still through the mouth
with the whispered sound of "Ha,"**

<u>the out - breath</u>
<u>is twice as long</u>
<u>as the in – breath.</u>

**For ease of mind:
try inhaling to 4 counts
while focusing on the crown**

**and then exhaling to 8 counts
while focusing on the navel area
and making the whispered
sound of "Ha"**

You can adjust the breath counts
to 3 - 6, 5 – 10,
6 -12, or whatever best suits
your natural breathing rhythm.

The Piko Piko Breathing
part is the focus on the crown
and the focus on the navel area
while inhaling and exhaling.

Practice this for 5 minutes
or, as long as you comfortably can.

When you are finished
with the "Ha" meditation technique
continue to sit quietly
and enjoy the deep stillness
and inhanced "energy" you feel.

As with the "Aloha" Meditation,
If you cannot sit comfortably,
this meditation can be done with eyes closed
while standing as well.

Please note:
because you are exhaling twice as long as you are
inhaling, one can tend to feel lightheaded or dizzy.

If this happens, stop and then begin again, when
this feeling subsides.

With practice, the lightheadedness or dizziness will begin to dissipate and then dissappear altogether.

Hawaiian Kahuna would do
the "Ha" meditation with Piko Piko Breathing
to gather and increase their mana (spiritual power)
before each blessing and/or healing.

They used "Ha," the breath of life, as a primary tool to strengthen and boost their spiritual power and spiritual energy before all ceremonies and sacred rituals.

Ho'oponopono

Ho'oponopono (ho-o-pono-pono) is an ancient Hawaiian practice of reconciliation and forgiveness.

Ho'oponopono means to make right.
It means to make right with others, that which is not in correct balance and alignment.
And/or to make right with whatever situation or circumstances - that are not in correct balance or alignment in your own life.

Ho'oponopono is a means to create or recreate harmony and a sense of unity with all life,

This Ho'oponopono technique is one method or practice. There are other forms of Ho'oponopono as well.

The beauty of this Ho'oponopono Meditation
is its simplicity.

The Ho'oponopono Meditation is a dynamic meditation that asks you to focus on four different expressions and the feelings behind them.

The four expressions are as follows:

I'm sorry

Please forgive me

I love you

Thank you

To begin: sit comfortably with a straight back, and close your eyes. Take 4 deep breaths, relax and start repeating these phrases either mentally or out loud.

There are no rules on how to repeat the phrases. You can say them in any order.

You can say all four phrases one after the other, and then begin again.

You can repeat the first phrase several times, then switch to the next phrase and repeat it several times, etc. and then start again from the beginning.

The essential part of this meditation is to feel the feelings, feel the intention behind each expression, as you focus on each person, or persons, or the situation or circumstances, that you would like to bring reconciliation, forgiveness, and healing towards.

The effect of this meditation can be profound. You may find it most beneficial to finish with the "Thank you" or "I love you" phrase.

With earnest and sincere application of this meditation, you will find your vibration (consciousness) rises; your clarity improves; and the qualities of forgiveness and compassion begin to melt away all the burdens of your heart.

It is best to do this meditation
first thing in the morning,
and just before bed in the evening,

or while stressed out
about a person or situation.

It is especially powerful while visiting a sacred site or heiau (Hawaiian Temple) that has the energy of healing and forgiveness, i.e. Pu'uhonua o Honaunau.

The four phrases can be also be said as an affirmation, rather than a meditation.
They can be repeated anytime, anywhere, and under all circumstances (although best to do them silently when others are around.)

A Hawaiian Blessing Chant
(English translation)

This blessing chant too, can be repeated anywhere, anytime, and under all circumstances. It is offered with variants, use according to your inspiration or need:

I am aware... I am free... I am focused... I am here (now)... I am loved [or I am happy]... I am strong [or I am confident]... I am healed [or I am positive]...

With strong focus and sincere application, this blessing can uplift, inspire, and empower.

The Bowl of Light - You are Spirit Greatness!

In Hawai'i, each child, as they were born, would have a bowl carved for them by one of the elders. It would be given to them and explained to them as they grew, that this bowl represented them.

The children were told that they were like bowls of shining light. They were "uhane nui" - spirit greatness. *All* humans are spirit greatness, and we shine from this place. We shine as spirit light.

And as we go through life, and things occur that are not pono, (correct and in balance) it is as if a pohaku (a rock) is put into the bowl. Eventually, if enough pohaku are put into the bowl, they block out the light and we can no longer shine, shine as spirit greatness – the way we were meant to be.

The Bowl of Light Ceremony with Native Hawaiian Stephanie Terlap and Kahuna Kalei'iliahi

The Hawaiians had a very simple solution for this: they would just huli (empty) the bowl, turn the bowl over - so all the rocks would fall out, so that they could continue to shine as the light of spirit – all that they were meant to be.

This is a very simple pragmatic practice.
A tool that if you wish to use, can be applied into your daily life, so that you can remain in your "spirit of greatness."

Use it, when incorrect actions that you created begin to feel overwhelming, and the bowl begins to feel heavy. You can huli the bowl, turn it over, so that all the rocks will pour out, so you can continue to shine your "light of greatness."

This is easily done using the

Bowl of Light Visualization:

Visualize that you are holding a Bowl of Light. That the Bowl of Light has become full of stones from incorrect actions that you have created. Slowly lift the bowl upwards and outwards about equal with the top of your head. Simply turn the bowl over, and let the stones fall. Visualize your bowl now full – filled with shining radiant light.

This is a simple and symbolic act of clearing your thoughts and energy, of purifying your emotions and your aura.

It is a way of leaving behind all those things that may separate you from receiving the fullest blessings in life.

The Intent of this Book...

The Aloha Spirit is Alive and Thriving!

Many are not aware of the ancient stories of creation and history revealed through the oral traditions of ancient Hawaiian (Mu) chant and song.

Most are only aware of Hawaiian history from the most recent migrations dating back to between 1,500 and 2,000 years ago.

The Hawaiian stories of creation and ancient history begin way before any known timeline generally understood and accepted today, perhaps millions of years.

This book was written to help bring crystal clarity and deep insight from a much higher viewpoint and much longer rhythm regarding the Aloha Spirit origins and the birth of the True Essence of Hawaiian Spirituality.

It is offered from sources of pure Hawaiian spiritual understanding and perspectives - beginning with and according to – ancient Hawaiian chants, songs, and oral history,

as Hawaiian true and pure spiritual essence IS found foremost in their chants, songs, and oral history.

Along with this, passed down across the ages and through generations of Hawaiian families, there are Hawaiian descendants, both in the past, and living today, whose specific role was/is to carry these traditions, teachings, and wisdoms forth.

Drawing from many living Hawaiians today, be they kahuna, kahu, healers, seers, light-carriers of Aloha, or, have in someway been responsible and entrusted to carry on and share these teachings and wisdom,

as well as drawing upon the ancient Hawaiian chants, songs and oral history, my hope and inspiration is to help create a new, deeper and more true understanding of the Aloha Spirit and the True Essence of Hawaiian Spirituality.

If, somehow, I have mistakenly included any incorrect information contained within the contents of this book, then, as is the Hawaiian and proper protocol, I fully apologize and claim sole responsibility for this oversight.

May you be deeply inspired,
And your journey be of abundant
and unceasing blessing!

Bibliography

David Kaonohiokala Bray and Douglas Low
The Kahuna Religion of Hawaii

Leinani Melville
Children of the Rainbow, The religion, legends and gods of pre-Christian Hawaii

Hank Wesselman
The Bowl of Light

King David Kalakaua
The Legends and Myths of Hawai'i

Queen Liliuokalani
Hawaii's Story by Hawaii's Queen Liliuokalani

William Ellis
A Narrative of an 1823 Tour of Hawai'i

W.D. Westervelt
Hawaiian Historical Legends

David Malo
Hawaiian Antiquities

Samual Kamakau
The Works of the People of Old

Peter H. Buck.
Arts and Crafts of Hawai'i (Religion)

About the Author:
Kahu Robert Kalama Frutos

Kahu Kalama is a wisdom keeper
of the true essence of Hawaiian spirituality and an
honored guardian of Hawai'i's sacred sites.

Kahu Kalama is also a spiritual intuitive,
healer, Aloha light carrier, visionary artist, esoteric
(soul) astrologer, internationally recognized
author/ camera artist, and earth guardian.

Tutored and mentored through the
years Kahu has trained with many of the foremost
Big Island Native Hawaiian cultural luminaries...
Kumu (teachers) Kapuna (elders) and Kahuna.

Kahu is multifaceted, talented, and spiritually
gifted, and has been hanaied (adopted) into the
spiritual & Hawaiian family of High Priestess
Kahuna Kalei'iliahi.

Kahu has been trained in Hawaiian healing
practices and given special permission to share
Hawaiian spirituality, healing, & the mana of

sacred sites by Kahuna Papa K.

Kahu has been encouraged and blessed to share the ancient Universal Hawaiian and Lumerian truths by Kumu Kahuna Nui Ehulani

Kahu Kalama is also the founder of the Light of Aloha Foundation, and Ministry, a not for profit educational venue for sharing spiritual inspiration, and techniques in practical spiritual living.

Kahu has created a unique body of work woven together from a broad spectrum of training and varied experience - a spiritual educator, internationally recognized author, counselor, professional camera artist, a successful multi - business owner, photo tour guide, sacred site tour guide, presenter, and healing practitioner.

Kahu offers support, encouragement, comfort, and assistance through mentoring, educating, intuitive counseling, and spiritual coaching - allowing you a fresh perspective (a view of the large picture), a clear sense of direction, and greater inner alignment.

Kahu possesses a great depth and passion that inspires you to realize that the spiritual world is not only possible but is an integral part of our everyday reality.

Kahu offers tours, classes, workshops, retreats, and private consultations. He has authored many books - including ***Hawai'i Sacred Sites of the Big Island Places of Wisdom Healing and Presence.***

His accomplishments provide insight into his passion, enthusiasm, and creativity. Kahu is a gifted teacher/speaker with a unique ability to easily share and communicate "how to live" practical spiritual living skills.

He also brings the same passion – into sharing the Spirit of Aloha, and the beauty, wonder, and magnificence of the Hawaiian Islands.

You can reach Kahu Kalama at:

www.hawaiisacredsitestours.com

www.hawaiiphototours.org

www.robertfrutos.com

email: rfphoto3@gmail.com

Phone: 808 345 – 7179

You can reach Kahuna(s) Kalei and Ehulani at:

Kahuna High Priestess Kaleiiliahi

http://www.kaleiiliahi.com/

Kumu Hula Ali'i Kahuna Nui Ehulani

http://www.hawaiianhuladance.com

Other Books by Robert Frutos

Clarity, Inspiration, & Optimum Potential: A Concise Guide for Creating Infinite Possibility in YOUR Life!

In the Pursuit of Excellence: A Concise Guide for Creating Unlimited Possibility in YOUR Life, Business and/or Organization!

Photographing Nature in Hawaii: Capturing the Beauty & Spirit of the Islands,

Hawai'i Inspiration Aflame: A Passion for the Magnificence,

Hawaii How to Capture the Dynamic Islandscape: A Photographers Approach,

A Photographer's Guide to Hawai'i Volcanoes National Park: Being in the Right Place, at the Right time, for the Best Image

With Beauty All Around Me: Inspirations to Touch the Heart, Heal and Uplift the Spirit

Walking in Beauty: Inspirational Seed Thoughts for Creating YOUR Best Life Possible

or more information about these books, go to:

www.hawaiisacredsitestours.com

Click on Robert's Links/Books

Lastly, I have one more photography book available, an inspiring coffee table book entitled: **Hawaii Inspiration Aflame: A Passion for the Magnificence**, for those who would like to see more extraordinary Hawai'i images, it includes images from some of the other Hawai'i islands as well.

This book is available directly from the author and the cost is $65.00, plus shipping. Email me at rfphoto3@gmail.com for more info./
to obtain a copy.

An Offering to Pele

Made in the USA
Charleston, SC
04 January 2017